# Gandhian Non-Co-operation

OR

# Shall India Commit Suicide?

# Gandhian Non-Co-operation

**OR**

# Shall India Commit Suicide?

## A VADE-MECUM

AGAINST NON - CO-OPERATION FOR ALL INDIAN PATRIOTS

GYAN

*Published by*

Gyan Publishing House
5, Ansari Road
Daryaganj, New Delhi-110002
Phone: 011-47034999, 9811692060
E-mail: books@gyanbooks.com

*Distribution Network*
gyanbooks.com
India, USA, Canada, UK, Australia



ISBN: 978-93-6433-280-4 (HB)

First Published, 1920

2nd Impression 2024

*Printed at:* Gyan Press, Delhi.



**GANDHIAN NON-CO-OPERATION**
**OR**
**SHALL INDIA COMMIT SUICIDE?**

# GANDHIAN NON-CO-OPERATION

OR

# SHALL INDIA COMMIT SUICIDE?

# Gandhian Non-Co-operation

OR

# Shall India Commit Suicide?

## A VADE-MECUM

Against Non-Co-operation for all Indian Patriots

Published by "New India" Office, Madras
Sold also at the Theosophical Publishing House, Adyar
Benares and Bombay (Medow Street, Fort)
1920

# FOREWORD

This booklet is a collection of articles, written by a number of well-known persons, against the fatal policy of Non-Co-operation, which is daily becoming more and more violent; if it be not checked by the resolute opposition of the thoughtful, it will crush the country by necessitating repression, or drive it into a welter of anarchy, a National suicide.

Mr. Gandhi, the leader of this crusade, has gone through a number of changes with bewildering rapidity. At the end of December, 1919, he proposed, but did not ultimately move, in the National Congress, a resolution promising Co-operation in reply to the King-Emperor's message, and finally agreed to a compromise resolution, not promising Co-operation, but directing the working of the Reforms with a view to obtain Self-Government.

In January, February and the first half of March, the attention of the country was focussed on the Reforms, and the political lectures delivered were directed towards educating the electorates for their new and responsible duties. Personally I worked hard at this, carrying on a regular campaign to popularise the Reforms. But side by side with this a movement grew up among the Musalmans, who became much disturbed over the Khilafat and Turkey, and Mr. Gandhi made common cause with them, and with them formulated his ultimately famous four progressive steps of Non-Co-operation.

A Khilafat Committee was formed early in 1920, and meetings were called to express sympathy with Turkey. On March 9 one was held in Madras, with the Hon. Mr. Yakub Hasan in the Chair, and Mr. Kasturiranga Iyengar, Mr. S. Satyamurti and many Hindu gentlemen were present. Mr. Montagu was praised by the Chairman, who said that he had suggested to him a powerful federation of Muslim States, which the British Government would help and with which it would co-operate. Resolutions were passed pledging unswerving loyalty and devotion to the Khalifa and stating that

> no terms that do not vouchsafe to the Turks the full and independent sovereignty over their Homeland in Europe and Asia, and to the Sultan the suzerainty over Arabia, Palestine, Syria and Mesopotamia, thus maintaining his position as Khalifa, the custodian and guardian of the Holy Places of Islam, can ever be acceptable to India that has helped the Allies to win the War.

A hartal was proposed for March 19, and Mr. Gandhi issued a manifesto strongly urging that there should be no violence and that it should be absolutely voluntary. He suggested that if the Turkish Treaty should be unsatisfactory, "there should be no violence in thought, speech, or deed, no boycott of British goods, as it is one form of violence, and no mixing of other questions with the Khilafat, such as the Egyptian question"; people holding offices of honour and emolument under Government and menial Government servants should resign. "Non-Co-opertion with the Government, free from all things of violence, is the only effective remedy open to the people." "No threat of ostracism should be used and the withdrawal of Co-operation should be purely voluntary." He spoke very strongly against violence:

> I should cease to co-operate and advise every Hindu and for that matter everyone else to cease to co-operate, the moment there was violence actually done, advised or countenanced. I would therefore urge upon all speakers the exercise of the greatest restraint under the gravest provocation. There is certainty of victory, if firmness is combined with gentleness. The cause is doomed if anger, hatred, ill-will, recklessness, and finally violence are to reign supreme. I shall resist them with my life, even if I should stand alone. My goal is friendship with the world, and I can combine the greatest love with the greatest opposition to wrong. (*New India*, March 10, 1920.) See also March 11.

Such was Mr. Gandhi in March, 1920.

Events thenceforth moved rapidly, Khilafat Committees were formed and meetings held. The Khilafat Offices in Calcutta were raided on March 14. The deputation which had gone to England with the Viceroy's help, kept in touch with India, and the crusade against the Turks in England during March embittered Musalman feeling in India; the Madras Provincial Congress Committee called on all to take part in the hartal of March 19, and some prominent Hindus and Musalmans in Madras issued a joint appeal (*New India*, March 17). here was a great and peaceful response all over India on March 19, and only in Burma was any repression used. *New India*, in a leading article on March 20, pointed out that underlying the Khilafat question was the question of European aggression on Asia, and that all Indians were one in objecting to Asian civilisation being engulfed by European, and in claiming equality for Asiatic and European.

A National Week, commemorating the Panjab atrocities was opened on April 6 by meetings at which all parties were represented. The main request made on April 6 was that the Rowlatt Act should be repealed; Mr. Gandhi declared at Bombay that if the Rowlatt Act were not repealed before the inauguration of the Reforms the demand made on them for Co-operation would be futile, and he, for one, would find the situation such as to make remaining within the Empire impossible (*New India*, April 7). The Khilafat does not appear to have been noticed in the resolutions passed; collections for the Jallianwala Bagh Memorial were pressed. But April 9, within the week, was fixed as "Khilafat Day," and on this a resolution was passed in Bombay and elsewhere, moved in Bombay by Mr. Gandhi, declaring that if the just demands of Musalmans were not agreed to,

> and in the event of any adverse decision being arrived at, it will be the duty of every Indian to withdraw Co-operation from Government until pledges are fulfilled and Muslim sentiment conciliated.

Thus was the fatal note struck, and the real Non-Co-operation campaign was begun on April 9, 1920.

In *The Citizen* of Madras and in *New India*, simultaneously, appeared, on April 10, Sir P. S. Sivaswami Iyer's article, "The Khilafat Situation," the first answer to the challenge; it is printed here on p. 3, as the opening article of our collection. On April 15, 16, 20 and 21 it was followed by Mrs. Annie Besant's four articles on "Co-operation or Non-Co-operation," and "Conscience," "The Present Crisis" and "A True Satyāgrahi," unfortunately overlooked when the collection was made; they are printed as an Appendix. The great Khilafat Demonstration in Madras was held on April 17, and Mr. Gandhi's famous four progressive steps in Non-Co-operation were passed as a resolution:

> In consonance with the spirit of the Resolution adopted by the All-India Khilafat Committee, this Conference, in the event of the present agitation proving futile and ineffective, calls upon all Indians to resort to progressive abstention from Co-operation with Government in the following manner:
>
> Firstly, to renounce all honorary posts, titles and memberships of Legislative Councils.
>
> Secondly, to give up all remuneratory posts under Government service.
>
> Thirdly, to give up all appointments in the Police and Military forces.
>
> Fourthly, to refuse to pay taxes to Government.

This was proposed by Moulvi Abdul Majid Sharar, seconded by Mr. S. Kasturiranga Iyengar, supported by Messrs. S. Satyamurti, C. Rajagopalachariar, A. Rangaswami Iyengar, M. K. Achariar, Pandit Bansi Dhar and several Musalmans. The President of the Conference, Moulana Shaukat Ali, added after reciting the four steps: 'We do not embark on this step without fully realising what it means. It means a movement for absolute independence." At that time, Mr. Gandhi did not go so far, but some of us clearly saw that the movement was definitely revolutionary, despite its sheep's clothing. From this time onwards *New India* kept up a fairly constant fusillade, and I wrote other articles in *The Citizen*, *The Servant of India*, *The Leader* and *The Looker-on*.

The Hon. Mr. V. S. Srinivasa Sastri joined in the fray on May 15 in *The Citizen*, and Mr. Jamnadas Dwarkadas—now a member of the Indian Legislative Assembly—in *The Bombay Chronicle*.

After the Congress the Hon. Mr. R. P. Paranjpe, Mr. C. P. Ramaswami Aiyar and I myself wrote in *The Servant of India*; Mr. Ambika Charan Mozumdar and later Sir A. Chaudhuri and Messrs. Satyananda Bose, J. N. Roy, J. Chaudhuri and B. C. Chatterji addressed the readers of *The Bengalee*; Mr. G. A. Natesan those of *The Indian Review*; the Hon. Mr. Bhurgri those of *The New Times*; and Mr. N. M. Samarth those of *The Asiatic Review*. Very many other articles must have appeared, and I should be grateful if any Editors who see this would send me on leaders from their papers, in case a second edition of this booklet should be needed.

The meeting of the All-India Congress Committee at Benares, on May 30 and 31, marked a new departure. It will be remembered that Mr. Gandhi, in March, had forbidden the mixing up of Non-Co-operation in defence of the Khilafat with other questions; but it was found that the Khilafat was not sufficiently attractive to Hindus so at Benares the Panjab Atrocities and the deficiencies of the Reform Act were added to the provocative causes. On June 1 at Allahabad, another grave addition was made—the creation of a Council, the directions of which were to be obeyed in action and abstention from action, practically a Council of War. An ultimatum was sent to the Viceroy, giving him a month's grace, and August 1 was proclaimed at the day on which Non-Co-operation was definitely to begin with Step No. 1. The response was poor, but fiery discussion went on all over the country.

On September 4, the Special Congress began, and after long discussion a resolution was formulated approving Mr. Gandhi's progressive policy, and amplifying Step No. 1 in detail. Over 3,000 delegates abstained from voting, 1,826 voted with Mr. Gandhi, 884 for Mr. Pal's amendment, and 63 objected to both or were neutral. The resolution was sent to a Sub-Committee of the All-India Congress Committee, amended by that body and published. Most of the Bengal, Madras and Bombay leaders, who had voted against Mr. Gandhi, submitted to the so-called "mandate" of the Congress on the Boycott of Council clause alone. A handful of lawyers have given up their practice; no one appears to boycott foreign goods. Mr. Gandhi himself uses railways, post, telegraph and motor cars. The failure of the propaganda has led to extraordinary violence of language, now passing into the breaking up of meetings. Mr. Gandhi and the two "Ali Brothers" in despair, have attacked Aligarh and Benares Universities and the Sikh Khalsa College. Aligarh has, after a struggle, held it own; no serious attack has been made on the other two, but Khalsa College has withdrawn from Government control.

The Liberals and National Home Rulers joined forces in educating the voters on the Reform Act, and have been actively co-operating against the dangerous Non-Co-operation Crusade.

This booklet is issued to give weapons to the combatants. The battle is joined, and as when the old knightly warriors charged, and met in shock of conflict, we cry with the Herald:

"GOD DEFEND THE RIGHT!"

*November 17, 1920* ANNIE BESANT

## CONTENTS

# BEFORE THE CONGRESS

# THE KHILAFAT SITUATION

By Sir P. S. Sivaswami Aiyar, K.C.S.I., C.I.E.

The agitation over the Khilafat question is now entering upon an acute phase and the course of action which has been proposed by Mr. Gandhi, and is evidently intended to be followed all over the country, cannot but cause grave concern to all who are interested in the welfare of India. The resolution which has been drafted by Mr. Gandhi for endorsement by public meetings on the 9th April expresses the hope that the Khilafat question will be solved consistently with the just demands of the Musalmans of India and the solemn pledges of His Majesty's ministers, and recommends that, in the event of any adverse decision being arrived at, every Indian should withdraw co-operation from the Government, until the pledges are fulfilled and Musalman sentiment conciliated. The extremely serious character of the step recommended renders it necessary that it should be examined in a calm and dispassionate spirit and that all its consequences should be clearly realised. The draft resolution itself does not specify the just demands of our Muhammadan countrymen, but it may be taken that they are embodied in the representation made by the Khilafat deputation at the interview with the Premier. The demands put forward related (1) to the custody of the holy places of Islam, (2) the control of the Jazirat-ul-Arab or the island of Arabia, and (3) the maintenance of the *status quo* with regard to Turkish sovereignty, so as to secure adequate temporal power to the Khalifa for the defence of the Faithful. Whether the religious requirements of Islam with regard to the first two demands would not be met by the recognition of Emir Feisul as King of Arabia is a point which is not altogether clear from the reply of Mr. Muhammad Ali. It is evident however, that the main ground of Musalman opposition to the proposals of the Peace Conference is that they will lower the power and prestige of the strongest surviving Muhammadan Empire in the world, and that the concession of independence to the backward nationalities of Arabia, Mesopotamia and Syria will not have the effect of erecting any strong Muhammadan Kingdom capable of resisting Christian-European aggression. It is not necessary for us to enquire whether the demands are based upon religious injunctions or upon racial or national sentiments. So far as the other communities in India are concerned it is sufficient for them to realise that their Muhammadan fellow-countrymen feel most strongly upon the subject, and that they have been greatly perturbed by the proposals for the dismemberment of Turkey. Whatever may have been the past attitude of the Musalmans towards the sacred places of Hinduism, their claim that the holy places of Islam should be under Muslim control and that the provinces of Turkey which are predominantly Turkish in race should remain subject to Turkish rule must command the sympathy of all right minded people. The Hindus have fully appreciated the feeling of the Muhammadans on this question and have extended their sympathy and support in their agitation so far. The proposal to cut off slices even from the territories of Thrace and Asia Minor which were admitted to be predominantly Turkish in race can hardly be reconciled with the solemn pledges given by the Premier in January, 1918. The proposal to apply the principle of self-determination to single cities like Smyrna certainly sounds extravagant. We do not know whether the proposal for the autonomy of essentially non-Turkish subject provinces within the limits of the Turkish Empire has received that careful examination which it deserves at the hands of the Peace Conference. But, whatever may be the justice of the demands of our countrymen, it is obvious from the reply of the Premier to the deputation, from the speeches in the British Parliament, from the comments of the English Press, and from the American Note, that the Turkish Empire will be dealt with by the Allies on lines which are not likely to be acceptable to our fellow-countrymen. The Government of India, the Secretary of State and the representatives of India at the Peace Conference have all steadily and strongly supported the Muhammadan view of the question and pressed it upon the attention of the Peace Conference and the English Cabinet. In some of the public meetings held by Musalmans during the last month, they expressed their unswerving *loyalty* and devotion to His Imperial Majesty the Sultan of Turkey as the Khalifa and Commander of the Faithful. Read with the other resolutions passed at these meetings, it sounds like a threat of severance of the ties of allegiance which bind the Musalmans of India to the British throne. Mr. Gandhi's resolution has probably been drawn up in the belief that the tendencies to lawlessness and violence will thereby be checked and diverted into constitutional channels; but is there the least likelihood of the agitation remaining within constitutional bounds or of its not involving any danger to society? Mr. Gandhi himself is a man of peace and abhors violence in any shape or form, but his own experience of the events of last year should have disillusionised him as to the capacity of the masses for self-control and their ability to confine their agitation within the limits of law and order. In April last year, Mr. Gandhi himself had to express his sorrow that, when he embarked upon a mass movement he underrated the forces of evil. Has the lapse of a year worked any miracle in human nature? The proposal to withdraw co-operation from the Government is couched in very general language. But let us analyse it and visualise all that it implies. So far as I have seen, the only person who has attempted to define the implications of this recommendation is Mr. Gandhi himself. In a manifesto published about the 11th March last he specifies some of the steps which would be involved in this campaign of Non-Co-operation. He recommends Non-Co-operation at the top and at the bottom and consequently the resignation of all offices of honour or ennoblement and all menial offices under the Government. It cannot be supposed that while he recommends the menial servants of the Government to give up their offices he intends to refer only to honorary offices at the other end of the scale. It would be attributing bad logic to Mr. Gandhi to suggest that he intended to exclude paid offices under the Government above the menial grade. Now, what does this lead to? It is nothing less than an exhortation of all officers in the civil employ of Government to strike work and do so for political reasons. It would include all Judges, Magistrates, all members of the Police force, all gaol officials and, in fact, officials in every department and every grade. Even if Mr. Gandhi's plans be not so comprehensive, strikes have a dangerously infectious tendency. We are also too familiar with the methods of strikers to believe that coercion will not be attempted against those who refuse to join in the strike. In judging of the character of any recommendation, we must proceed upon the assumption that it is sincerely intended and expected to be successful and not upon the assumption that it will fall flat and is intended or expected to be ineffective. Mr. Gandhi himself is the very soul of sincerity and means what he says, but there are some of our countrymen who think that, while proposals of this sort will not materialise and do any harm, they may do good by way of threat. It is absurd to believe that the authorities against whom such talk is indulged in cannot see through it. Let us then assume that there is a general political strike of all the civil officers in the employ of Government. The result will be that the whole administration will be paralysed and brought to a stand-still. Mr. Gandhi has not pronounced whether his programme of Non-Co-operation would permit or prohibit the payment of taxes. Logic requires prohibition. Mr. Gandhi stated in his manifesto that advice to the soldier to refuse to serve would be premature, that it would be the last and not the first step and that the people would be entitled to take that step when the Viceroy, the Secretary of State and the Premier deserted us. The Viceroy and the Secretary of State have done their level best. The Premier has refused to budge an inch from the conclusions of the Allies at the Peace Conference. Has the time then arrived for taking this step also? But, whether it has or not, the paralysis of the civil administration will be sufficient to bring about a state of anarchy and cause untold suffering and misery to the people. What is the object which has to be achieved at the cost of such frightfulness? It may be said that it is to bring the Government of India down on their knees and make them fall into line with the wishes of the Musalmans. Suppose the Government of India is willing, as it always has been in this matter, to act in conformity with the wishes of the Musalmans: what is the course of action that the Government of India have to take? They can only make a representation to the Imperial Government and to the Peace Conference and that they have done without being prompted thereto by any campaign of non-co-operation. What is the specific course of action that Mr. Gandhi would desire the Government of India to take? Are they to go to war against the United Kingdom or against the Allies, and if they are to be driven to any such extraordinarily absurd course, does anybody dream for a moment that the Musalmans of India or even all the populations of India are prepared or able to carry on a successful war against the Empire or the Allies, not to speak of America. Mr. Gandhi himself perceives the barbarousness and futility of any resort to violence by the people against the Government. Is not a resort to arms against the Empire and the Allies and in fact the whole of Christendom still more ludicrous? England will or may respond to appeals to her sense of honour and chivalry, but to suppose that she will be cowed down by threats or can be beaten is childish.

Harmless as the word "Non-Co-operation" may at first look, it is bound to bring the people into collision with the Government and to end in active resistance and rising against the Government. Any Government worthy of the name must, so long as it exists, discharge its primary duty of maintaining order, which would necessarily involve the employment of methods of repression against the forces of lawlessness. The only result that I can foresee of this ill-advised campaign is that it will recoil upon the people either by the introduction of anarchy and lawlessness or by the employment of repressive measures and in either case, the clock of progress will be set back for generations to come. The doctrine of Non-Co-operation has a sinister affinity to the doctrine of passive resistance of which we heard not long ago. But, whatever justification there may be in extreme cases of internal maladministration, they would be quite unsuitable where the grievance relates to international problems. It cannot be too clearly pointed out that the cause of this agitation is nothing connected with the internal administration of our country, and that our religious observances, worship or rights in this country have in no way been interfered with. Even in the case of our own countrymen who have settled in Africa and whose civil rights have been infringed and threatened by the white settlers, nobody has ever suggested the employment of coercion against our own Government. The employment of the method of campaign now advocated by Mr. Gandhi and our Musalman friends, for the purpose of settling an international problem and in a manner apparently against the wishes even of the Muslim populations in the regions affected, is altogether indefensible.

In all disputes between men in this world there is a limit up to which alone they can be possibly carried by appeals to tribunals or otherwise. In political and international disputes the last resort is to arms. Turkey chose to enter the war needlessly and wilfully and was worsted in the arbitrament. Strenuous efforts have been made by the authorities in India, the Secretary of State and of India's representatives at the Peace Canference to secure by diplomacy generous treatment for Turkey. Should they fail, it would indicate the need for cessation of agitation in this country. In his interview with the Premier, Mr. Muhammad Ali expressed the hope of reconciling Turko-Arab differences and of persuading Emir Feisul that his own ambitions and those of the Arabs could be entirely satisfied within the scheme of Turkish sovereiguty. Here would seem to be a most promising direction for propagandist work and peaceful persuasion. Could Mr. Muhammad Ali and his colleagues persuade the Arabs to appreciate the advantages of Turkish rule and demand the restoration of Turkish rule or at any rate of Turkish suzerainty, there would be no likelihood of the League of Nations or any individual Power interposing any obstacles to the satisfaction of the demand.

After the most anxious consideration and with every sympathy for the views of our Musalman friends, I find it impossible to come to any other conclusion than that the adoption of the campaign of Non-Co-operation will be fraught with disaster to the country. It has caused me no little pain to be obliged to criticise the proposals which have been put forward by Mr. Gandhi, a person for whose saintly character and lofty ideals I have always entertained the highest respect. It is because I feel that the agitation is heading towards a cataract that I have considered it my duty to sound a note of warning. I have only to add that I am expressing these views in my individual capacity and not on behalf of any organisation—*The Citizen.*

---

## NON-CO-OPERATION

By the Hon. Mr. V. S. Srinivasa Sastri

Mr. Gandhi handles the affairs of individuals and of nations with the directness and detachment of the ascetic. He strips all questions, big and small, of their trappings and gets to their core at once. No sophistries can deceive, no irrelevancies distract, his logic. As his mind deals with a few simple essential categories, his language admits of no ambiguities or subtleties. With him to see a duty clearly is to pursue it unflinchingly. Sacrifice and suffering do not matter when they affect him only. When they affect others, his heart feels a pang, but his course persists like a force of nature. Is society convulsed and sore? It is a pity, but we must press on for that way lies *satya*. When a hero is bent on an ideal, he will not listen to a calculation of the cost. Justice, honour, truth—these are imponderable. Human lives and human happiness are nothing in comparison, though in their own sphere they need not be despised. Mr. Gandhi has persuaded himself that the Khilafat is a just and great cause and calls on his countrymen to win it under his banner or die. Unlike soldiers in a mercenary or conscript army, each one of us, to whom the appeal is addressed, has a right and a duty to examine the matter for himself before deciding what answer to give.

On the religious aspect of the Khilafat no non-Muslim has the right to hold an opinion of his own. I will not presume to say a word under that head or as to the practical bearing of the texts of the Koran dealing with the matter. The facts of history, however, have a significance which any student can appreciate. It has been asserted that the Khalifa of Islam was for a long period without any temporal power and his spiritual office was confined within very narrow limits; that the Sultan of Turkey assumed the Khilafat at a date comparatively recent; that he has no indefeasible title to it apart from the consent or acquiescence of the Islamic powers; that he does not belong to the tribe to which the Khalifa must belong; that the Musalmans of India, whether belonging to the ruling dynasties or private citizens, acknowledged the Sultan as Khalifa only fifty to sixty years ago. When I give due weight to these statements, for which high authority can be cited, I am inclined to appreciate the secular loss to the Islamic peoples involved in the extinction of their last great kingdom rather than the outrage to their religious feelings. The main strength of their case seems to rest on the pledge given by the Prime Minister of Great Britain, a pledge which is to be treated as idle breath because of the rich oil fields of Mosul and similar temptations. The League of Nations is heralded into being in an atmosphere of greed and self-aggrandisement on the part of the Powers that profess to have gained liberty and self-determination for mankind. This surely is the greatest tragedy that history has yet seen on this planet. But every great conception has only slowly been embodied in enduring institutions. The brotherhood of man is an ancient idea, but how far are we yet from having realised it? I agree with Mr. Gandhi in condemning the violation of Mr. Lloyd George's promise. But I do not agree with him in considering the people of India in any sense a party to the wrong. In a constitutional sense the majority of the voters in Great Britain (not the people even there) may be held responsible for their Prime Minister's actions. We in India are not responsible at all, not even for the actions of the Government of India. And this Government stands clear and without blemish in this affair. Mr. Gandhi says: "Co-operation must be withdrawn because the people must not be party to a wrong." I cannot, I confess, see the obligation resting on me to withdraw co-operation from a Government which has done right in order to influence another Government which has done wrong, merely because the former is politically subordinate to the latter. The whole argument is fantastic to a degree. Equally untenable and ingenious is the position that Non-Co-operation is not anti-government. An organised movement on the part of subjects, to be executed in four stages each more effective than the preceding, intended to embarrass at first and then utterly paralyse the machinery of Government, until not that Government but a Superior Government six thousand miles away is "compelled" to give redress—is it anything but an abuse of language to say that such a tremendous popular upheaval is "not anti-government"? Mr. Gandhi proceeds to claim that the movement is "logical and harmless". I cannot agree that it is logical as I dispute the premisses. As to its being harmless, I will readily grant that Mr. Gandhi wishes it to be so, and will abandon it without compunction when it ceases to be so. The wish is idle in view of the feelings brought into exercise, and the religious injunctions operating on the minds of the people principally affected. Mr. Gandhi may be justified in expecting strict compliance with his pacific commandments from those that have been in living contact with his personality in his āshrama and assimilated its discipline. Is he not incurring grave risks and grave responsibilities when he expects the same compliance from casual Satyagrahins who submit to his rule for a certain purpose under the stress of an overpowering emotion, who feel that in a way they are not obeying their own religion in submitting to that rule, and who will naturally give play to their own impulses the moment they become impatient? I know the answer. "To the extent the people remain under my control," Mr. Gandhi will say, "they are out of harm's way. It is so much gained." Elsewhere he has stated: "To do nothing is to invite violence for a certainty." In another place he implies that the intensity of Muslim resentment is not appreciated in its fulness by the arm-chair politicians who seem to believe that, if let alone, the resentment will soon die away. I am not always rocking in an arm-chair and do not underrate Muslim feeling. But I cannot altogether suppress the thought, which is daily growing to be a conviction, that Mr. Gandhi's advocacy has given the outraged feeling of the Muhammadan community a degree of strength, justification and authority which it would otherwise have lacked, and brought to its aid the active support of sections of the non-Muslim communities. It is difficult now to speculate on what might have happened if Mr. Gandhi had not identified himself with the Khilafat movement. Many who wish to judge the situation fairly may believe that, without improving its final chances of success in international counsels, he has but added to its vogue, strength, and potentialities for mischief. Of course, he has no such belief or intention, that goes without saying. Those who are of this way of thinking will not be ready to exonerate him from responsibility when he abandons the movement on account of its getting out of control, should it ever do so, which God forbid.

Another proposition laid down by him seems likewise open to question. It shows in a clear light the difference in dynamic quality between the convictions of a person like Mr. Gandhi and those of mere men of the world. He says Non-Co-operation will be a test of the sincerity of the Hindu profession of friendship. The test is too hard. I call myself a friend of the Musalman people. I believe they have a very sore grievance. I fear the settlement of the Turkish question will be in the nature of a broken pledge. I sympathise with them and am prepared to support their case in all reasonable ways. But I cannot support them in the policy of Non-Co-operation or in their threatened withdrawal of allegiance. They may say my friendship and support are not of much value. But I claim they are sincere. My reading of history does not sustain the claim that they set up in its entirety. I do not believe in the efficacy of their methods and apprehend serious danger from them. Lastly, the Koran has laid no commandments on me, and even the high authority of Mr. Gandhi fails to convert me to the theory that fellow-citizenship includes an unrestricted obligation to suffer for a religion not one's own.—*The Citizen*.

---

## NON-CO-OPERATION

### A CRY FOR HALT

By Jamnadas Dwarkadas, M.L.A.

I do not think any apology is needed from me if I, without any reserve, express my views on the methods of advancing the just cause of Muslims with regard to the Khilafat. As I shall show, apology is rather due from those leaders, who, from mixed motives, have studiously refrained from expressing their views and allowing their silence to be construed as evidence of support towards contentious resolutions taken in the name of the Nation. In Saturday's (Bombay) *Chronicle*, its special correspondent announced the direct initiation of the "Non-Co-operation campaign" as a "historic Hindu-Moslem decision". From the resolution of the All-India Congress Committee to refer the question to a special session of the Congress, I gathered that the question was held over for subsequent decision. It is true the All-India Congress Committee evaded decision for fear of its being unfavourable to "Non-Co-operation," as leaders even like Mr. Tilak and Lala Lajpat Rai expressed themselves against immediate adoption of the movement, and pointed out the practical difficulties that were in the way. However, if the special session is held at Calcutta, we shall have the opportunity of submitting Mr. Gandhi's proposals to the judgment of the Congress which claims to express National opinion. Decisions, so far reaching have to be thoroughly discussed by representative bodies, before being expressed in the name of the Nation and as an injunction to the people. What makes for immediate popularity now is not candour, but diplomatic silence. When I say that before the movement is directly launched the opinion of leaders ought to be ascertained and published for open criticism, I hope I shall not be accused of attempting tactics for delay. I hope my sympathies will not be doubted. I feel deeply for our Muslim brethren who are justly distressed over the iniquity of the Turkish Treaty. It is a treaty of spoliation, calculated to wreck the prospects of revived Islamic culture, and entirely to disrupt the religious policy of Islam. To Muslims, the sole justification for existence, is their religion; and their religion enjoins upon them to maintain the integrity of the Khalifa. What is the use of the British Government repeatedly saying, with an air of tolerance, that the question of the Khilafat is one for Muslims to decide? When they have a hand in depriving the Khalifa of his attributes, of his wardenship of the Holy Places, they are guilty of meddling with a sacred institution, and there is no sincerity in their ostentatiously offering the question for the judgment of Muslims. Professions of non-interference seem to me to be rather hollow, and I can understand the anguish of Muslims as they watch, in impotence, the degradation of a vital institution. Again, I feel as much as Mr. Gandhi does, that there have been, in the Treaty, flagrant violations not only of the principle of self-determination, but also of pledges made by Mr. Lloyd George and Lord Hardinge and recently confirmed by the Premier, as binding on the British Nation. Compliance with secret treaties, the lure of oil, the grab of untrustworthy claimants like Greece after the Smyrna atrocities, the threatened hectoring of the King of Syria in spite of the Damascas Congress, the promotion of tribal antagonisms—all these form a discredited chapter in European diplomacy. Muslims no doubt feel indignant that the fate of a sacred office should have become the sport of Imperialistic grab. All Indians share their feelings, sick as they are that a treaty so outrageous should be accompanied by humanitarian professions. Lastly, there is the menace of the rank exploitation of all Asiatic peoples demonstrated in the Treaty. This threat and foretaste of vassalage, fairly accomplished in Africa, adds to the indignity of a peace, which would have been softer if the vanquished Nation had been Christian and European. As it is, the dismemberment of Turkey by the Powers is a crime of the type of the partition of Poland, only the results will, unless the wrongs are duly repaired, be more disastrous in their nature.

I have dwelt at length on the nature of the Turkish Treaty, to show that I fully sympathise with the anguish of Muslims, and regard the fate of the Khilafat as a calamity. I am anxious that no means should be lost for remedying a wrong so gross, and so potent with the forces of evil reaction. Mr. Gandhi has devised the Non-Co-operation movement; the meeting of the All-India Central Khilafat Committee held in Bombay on May 12, accepted it for trial; and now it is announced as a "joint decision of Hindus and Moslems". Before the initiation of even the first of the four stages, I must be permitted to point out that Muslims should requisition their leaders to express their opinion on the operation of the movement. Surely it is not an extravagant demand to make. At the meeting in Bombay on May 12, at which I was present and expressed my views against the movement, out of 54 members from Bombay not even half a dozen were present to adopt the final decision. We have a right to ask that Muslim opinion should be fairly well consolidated before general action is decided upon. Hitherto, on questions affecting the Muslims of India, the All-India Muslim League used to represent their cause and confer with the Congress. The League at Amritsar passed strong resolutions protesting against the threatened position of Turkey and the degradation of the Khalifa. On the methods of subsequent agitation they pronounced no opinion. Now, while the Congress Committee is asked to decide the question, the Committee of the League, hitherto respected as the organ of authentic Muslim opinion, remains silent. As if to improve the puzzle of inaction on the part of reputed leaders, men like Mr. Jinnah, Mr. Hasan Imam, Mr. Mazahrul Haque, and the Raja of Mahmudabad are silent. Mr. Jinnah is the President of the League and a distinguished Muslim leader; he has been silent and unfound whenever the non-co-operation question is discussed. The Raja of Mahmudabad is the ex-president. Mr. Bhurgri, who presided over the Provincial Khilafat Conference, has, by way of protest, renounced his seat on the Council, while expressly rejecting and unequivocally condemning the new doctrine of "Non-Co-operation". Why is it, that the Muslim League does not express an opinion for the better guidance of others? How is one to explain the culpable silence of leaders whose opinions we ought to know? I do not set much store by any *firman* of Muslim Princes. But Indian Muslims who are free agents and qualified to express opinions ought to come forward abandoning the attitude of ambiguity. This is not an occasion for temporising in silence. I quite respect the attitude of Maulvi Azar-Subhani, who was definite about scriptural obligation, as he spoke at the Allahabad Conference. We were told by Maulvi Muhammad Ali at Allahabad, that "Non-Co-operation" was adopted by way of concession to Hindus who may not wholly agree with the mandates of the Koran. Two clear facts ought to be distinguished in the functions at Allahabad. The first is the attendance of Hindus at the invitation of Muslims and the expression of general sympathy from all parts of the country, so far as the terms of the Treaty are concerned. Hindu sympathy is firm and unequivocal. I had almost said that the firmness of some Hindus should be an example to the waverings of some Muslims. However, that may be, the joint meeting was utilised for an exposition of the Koranic doctrine, and later a free discussion of issues. The report says that "some" differed as to the remedy suggested, "some" welcomed it in principle, "some" expressed doubts as to its success. This is very unsatisfactory to go upon, and the reference to "some" is far too casual for a subject of such importance. The only mention of opposition is in the name of Mrs. Besant. I may be wrong in giving out names, but I ought to say that almost all the visitors were, for one reason or another, sceptical of the immediate value of "Non-Co-operation". It is to me strange to be told with reference to the discussion that the general feeling was in favour of "Non-Co-operation". My second point is that the meeting at which the "Non-Co-operation" resolution was adopted consisted of Muslims who alone voted, discussions being over. If, therefore, the reporter had alluded to "historic Hindu-Moslem *discussion*" instead of "historic Hindu-Moslem *decision*," I for my part should not have complained of false description.

I was, not long ago, criticised for speaking at a public meeting in favour of "Non-Co-operation" and some days later dissociating myself from the movement. I may say at once, that when I supported the resolution at the Bombay meeting which by the way was called during the Jallianwala Bagh week, for the purpose of commemorating the date on which Hindu-Muslim relations were cemented last year, I honestly believed that after last year's experience Mr. Gandhi would refrain from proposing a resort to another form of

Satyāgraha, especially because in this instance, Muslims were concerned. Having resigned from the Satyāgraha Sabhā last year, because of Mr. Gandhi's intention to resume civil disobedience, I can scarcely be expected to support it only in another form again. This step brought on me a good deal of criticism and unpopularity especially among Mr. Gandhi's followers, who subsequently strangely acquiesced in Mr. Gandhi's decision not to start it again. As a matter of fact, although the Rowlatt Act unfortunately still remains on the Statute Book, civil disobedience is, I take it, permanently given up. With regard to the renunciation of titles, which was on the programme, I am still in favour of its being carried out entirely on its own merits, and as a legitimate demonstration of our protest. I believe titles and honours have a very demoralising effect on our public life, and we should not be, in any way, losers if we abandoned them. As a matter of fact it was a relief to me to discover at the All-India Congress Committee that even Mr. Tilak and Lala Lajpat Rai who, according to Mr. Shaukat Ali's information to me on the 12th of May approved of the movements, had not given their unqualified support to the movement.

I am glad that as soon as I knew of the further ramification of the movement I expressed my scepticism, and that is my position still, only, with this difference, that as time passes I see more of danger in the movement and less of advantage. My only wish is that the public must not labour under any illusion through the silence or ambiguous expressions of leaders.

The scheme of "Non-Co-operation" on which Mr. Gandhi relies is a hazardous experiment, which is not in any visible manner fitted on to the end in view, which is the revision of the Turkish Treaty. To give up titles and honours is good. The resignation of honorary offices in the Legislative Councils would be doubtful as a measure considered by itself. The member who represents a constituency is under its authority, and he is not primarily a servant of the Crown. He would be serving his own people, however humble his opportunities may be. In their absence in India, substitutes, perhaps less efficient and less trustworthy, are sure to be found. That would admittedly be a disaster. I believe Mr. Gandhi also includes in the first stage, the giving up of sanads by lawyers as naturally they co-operate with His Majesty's Judges in administering law. Apart from this step being impracticable —and will my friends who are Muslim lawyers openly disagree with me on this question by giving up their sanads ?—in which case the movement could end in a fiasco; assuming that it did succeed, it could not but end in destroying the rightful protection of the citizen.

The cessation of voluntary payments must include the boycott of the postal service, telegraphs, and perhaps also of railways. If that is reached, communications even to ensure the success of the proposed organisation of volunteers would become impossible. The fact is that some disconnected acts of mortification are put together by Mr. Gandhi and called "Non-Co-operation".

Next is the resignation of Offices. Here the least that may be asked is that those in high position and able to judge for themselves should, if at all, set the example before poorer employees are invited to do it. May I suggest that the proposal should be made to all, from Mr. Ameer Ali, the oldest of Muslims in British service, down to Mr. Wazir Hasan, ex-secretary of the Muslim League and the latest among His Majesty's judges. I do not write in jest but in all seriousness. As was rightly pointed out both by the Hon. Pandit Madan Mohan Malaviya—than whom Muslims cannot imagine a better Hindu friend—and the Hon. Dr. Tej Bahadur Sapru, it would be a crime to ask subordinate employees to resign before those holding high offices have set an example. Supposing this step is of doubtful success, Mr. Gandhi would proceed to the third stage consisting of the resignation of police and military forces. If this swells a large crowd of the hungry and the unoccupied premised in the second stage, they no doubt must have a free hand, which in the absence of check may degenerate into free-bootage in spite of the hypothesis of non-violence. The non-payment of taxes would then seem simple, as the authorities would be without the power of summoning the defaulters through lack of public service. I hope I am not caricaturing Mr. Gandhi's programme, but it strikes me as an unnecessarily circuitous method of dislocating the functions of the State and paralysing Government, to the detriment of public safety and peace. But the greatest danger comes when all these may be proved unworkable, for the manifesto of the Khilafat Committee lays down as follows :

"Finally the Musalmans desire to observe that whilst they expect full success through the peaceful method of 'Non-Co-operation,' they realise that either through Hindu apathy or disunion amongst Musalman ranks, 'Non-Co-operation' may fail to achieve the end. In that case and no other the Musalmans reserve to themselves the right to take such other and further steps as may be enjoined upon them by their religion for the purpose of securing a satisfactory solution of the Khilafat question."

I should entreat Mr. Gandhi to draw for himself a mental picture of the India that might be when this stage is reached. Will not the wrath of an angry people turn alike on friends and foes? I shudder to think of the contingencies of this last phase as indicated in the passage quoted above.

I know that while I discuss the objective chain of events, Mr. Gandhi's eye is fixed on the conquering power of soul force! If this had concerned Mr. Gandhi as an individual very few in the world would have had the right to advise him. Because I may assert with a fair amount of accuracy that Mr. Gandhi personally, as a saint and a martyr, is one of the few triumphs of humanity. But may I point out with equal candour that Mr. Gandhi is making the error of a personal experience as being a workable achievement for the untutored who in their enthusiasm subscribe to the formula? Apart from the company of pledged though undisciplined workers, who invite suffering, we have to reckon with the existence of the large and indeterminate body of camp-followers less amenable to restraints than others. Even without aspersing the motives of any, it is surely possible to draw attention to this vital consideration. Even last year Mr. Gandhi publicly affirmed that he had underrated the forces of evil in launching his movement, and that he was the only person fitted to discharge its responsibilities. That in fact is what I myself wrote when severing my connection with the Satyāgraha Sabhā last year. Here it is:

"I may add here that I am saying all this in the spirit of a lover of Satya and Ahimsa, the two fundamental principles on which Satyāgraha is based. I believe that law-breaking can be practised by one who is a law unto himself, even such a one as Mr. Gandhi is, one who has understood God's laws, and to whom any infringement of them, be it by the Government or by his own people, is equally intolerable."

While I write like this, it may be asked what alternative remedy I have for meeting the religious obligations of the Khilafat. I am not very clear, about the solution, but, even if I do not say what occurs to me as a good beginning, I should be right in pointing out what is palpably wrong. Mr. Gandhi's method is perhaps in the opinion of a few Muslims, something to cling to in the absence of other proposals. But it is inappropriate and probably disastrous, even in the early stages of its operation. I am very much concerned to point out that the decisions taken by a few, genuine and zealous as they are, should not be expressed as a joint decision of the two communities, when some leaders are silent and others are dissuading us from the step. The Turkish Treaty is too top-heavy in its injustice to last long. Whatever the Congress may decide and the Muslims adopt, we ought to retain it as an All-India question and keep the agitation alive. Now the combination of European Governments is too trustful of physical force in the Middle Eastern settlement. These Governments will not last for ever. Juster appreciation of the Peace Treaty, there will be. And if we acquaint the British and European public with the rapacity of the Turkish Treaty, we may, when more democratic Governments come, prevail upon them to voluntarily disgorge their ill-gotten gains. Let us for at least two years keep up the agitation within constitutional limits, as we did at the time of the Partition of Bengal, another settled fact. If we organise ourselves in better union and realise the power of concerted action in the economic and commercial sphere, we may succeed in reminding Britain of the stern offence she has given to India by countenancing the wrong of despoiling lands got mainly through Indian valour. Let us be chary of abrupt steps and strange remedies that do not satisfy the reason, and that cost the ordinary unregenerate too much while helping them. Supporters of "Non-Co-operation" are doing a grave disservice to the country; those who, knowing their own minds, are silent are doing their followers a gross injustice; and let me add, those who oppose it are probably earning the anger and opprobrium of a certain section of the public. Even public journals that ought to speak out are in a state of deferential dissembling, sure of the outcome, but prefering to wait and flow with the current.

Let me, in conclusion, recall the moral of last year's events. The agitation against the Rowlatt Act was gathering force and when all might have worked for its early repeal, the issue of civil obedience brought direct and united agitation to a standstill. Union gave place to a breach of solidarity. Parties set themselves on the promotion and discouragement of civil disobedience, obscuring the possibility of retaining union and adding internal momentum to constitutional agitation. The fight for the repeal of the Act was diverted, and it become an internecine controversy among Indians themselves. For the bureaucrat, the opposition became less formidable. Officials could call for sympathy from a section of the people, who were left between the duty of agitating for repeal and the responsibility of resisting the practice of civil disobedience. In the Khilafat agitation, we shall have gained immensely if we retain the solidarity of the protest and add strength to it by methods which do not alienate any section of the people, or turn the issue into one of the immediate preservation of public tranquillity. My opinion is that by a hazardous attempt for narrow intensity, we may be sacrificing the prospect of a unique and well-organised agitation in India for a right cause. The marks of separation in the ranks through fear of being overcarried in the venture, without proportionate certainty of success, are becoming visible; and it is not necessary to pursue the argument further to demonstrate the gravity of this particular risk in mobilising power for the cause.—*The Bombay Chronicle.*

---

## IS THERE A WAY OUT?

By Annie Besant

Every one who objects to Non-Co-operation is asked, not unnaturally: "What do you propose *to do*." If, as many of us believe, the path of Non-Co-operation leads straight to a precipice, there is reason enough for objecting to it, *per se*, in that falling over a precipice is fatal. I submit that Non-Co-operation, in aim and in method, is revolutionary, for it aims at overthrowing the Government, and its method is by the force of numbers, thus "bringing it to its knees". A Government ceases to exist *qua* Government, whether you seize its members, imprison or execute them, or deprive them of all power by paralysing them, so that they cannot function. The object is the same: to compel the Government to submit by depriving it of the exercise of its powers. It will be admitted, I presume, that both a Jehad and Sinn Fein are revolutionary. Non-Co-operation is said by Muslims to be "a form of Jehad". *Young India*, in an editorial note, said that the difference between Sinn Fein and Non-Co-operation was that the former used violence and the latter did not. It would therefore seem that, by the statements of its leaders, Non-Co-operation is essentially revolutionary.

I do not deny that a Nation is justified in overthrowing a Government, when its yoke becomes intolerable. All free Nations admit this right, and all of them have, at some stage of their history, exercised it. The question thus becomes: "Is the British yoke so intolerable that it should be broken by revolution?" This is the bed-rock of difference between the neo-Nationalists, and the pre-1918 Congress-Nationalists; both aim at making India a Free Nation, but the second use reforms as their means, while the first in their acceptance of Non-Co-operation, use revolution. Everyone who seeks for India Self-Government as a Free Nation within the Empire, is a Nationalist in the real meaning of the word, and I have always denied the claim of the Extremists to monopolise it. But practically the second consists of Moderates, Liberals, and National Home Rule Leaguers, while the first comprehends the "Congress Party," the Extremists, and apparently the All-India Home Rule Leaguers.

Is the British yoke so intolerable as to justify revolution, whether by force of arms or by Non-Co-operation? I deny it. The Local Government in the Panjab, with Sir Michael O'Dwyer at its head, was intolerable, and the atrocities under Martial Law were intolerable. No words can be too strong in their denunciation, and the supineness of the Central Government in carrying out the directions of the Imperial Government is most blameworthy, the penalties imposed on General Dyer are inadequate, and the defence of him in the House of Lords adds one more to its many sins against Justice and Liberty. But against these, we must put the rule over the rest of India during these troublous times. Bombay may well be cited against the Panjab, Sir George Lloyd against Sir Michael O'Dwyer. The wounds of Bengal have been largely healed by the Royal amnesty, and its use in the Panjab has given her back the political leaders of whom Sir Michael O'Dwyer had deprived her. A few years ago newspapers were destroyed for a tithe of the freedom which they now exercise unchallenged, and men were imprisoned for far less than is said unhindered on many a platform to-day. I do not think that most people recognise the immense change of spirit which has come over the administration; their minds are so full of the Panjab cruelties that they do not see the present enlarged area of liberty, and in their righteous indignation with the malefactors of 1919, they do not recognise the honest efforts of the Governments of 1920. The continuance of Panjab misrule and its spread over India would have justified revolution: the change in the Panjab and the large changes in India would make revolution a crime.

I say "would have justified revolution," but must add, "if possible and beneficial". As things are, revolution would mean anarchy, and would result in a new foreign ruler infinitely worse than the old. For India has no army, no navy. She cannot defend her own frontiers, and, reduced to anarchy, with no government and no discipline, she would fall an easy prey to any armed Nation. Britain has sinned against India in holding back substantial reforms for so long, in narrowing them too much even when given, and above all, in not fulfilling the ruler's first duty of protection by the condign punishment of those who, in the words of the Secretary of State's Despatch, treated those who had the right to look to them for protection as though they were enemies. These are great sins and they have—it is idle to blink the fact—estranged the Nation, and made many look with half-approval on suggestions of ending the British connection. But Britain has also great virtues, and Co-operation with her will bring India more swiftly to fully responsible government than any other line of action.

Let us look facts in the face. India is weak, because divided; helpless, because unarmed. Non-Co-operation is a big gamble, with anarchy as one stake and utter futility as the other. It must fail, because counsels are opposed. What is the use of banging the table and saying that no honest Indian *must* enter the Councils, when candidates are thronging to every constituency? It is futile to say without power or authority: you *must*, when candidates reply: "We won't." Orators cannot prevent them from going to the polls; they can abuse them, but abuse has been so overdone that it now falls flat.

What then is the way out? I fear there is only one sure way, for even resolutions, protests, meetings, will soon be overborne by the pressing interest of the elections. None the less, they should not be despised, for all we have gained so far has been the result of these now-condemned methods of constitutional agitation, and even now the Central Government is being pushed by it into action, inadequate though that action be. There is only one way, because others are barred. Revolution by violence is inexpedient and impossible. Revolution by non-violence, Non-Co-operation, leads either to anarchy or futility. What is left? Working to get our very best men into the Councils. Sending up from every Council a resolution demanding justice on the offending officials of the Punjab and for compensation to their victims, with the annulment of all sentences and refund of all fines; a resolution demanding the repeal of all emergency legislation in connection with disturbances, including sedition and treason in speech: the passing of a Bill abolishing the sex disqualification for the political franchise, so as to enlist the great force of Indian-womanhood for the public benefit; the using of every power for improving the condition of the masses, by local self-government, education, improvements in agriculture, industries, and the like. The first resolution will be for the healing of the past, the second for the guarding of the future. The legislation will be for the uplift of the masses, for the removal of the poverty which is strangling India to death.

To the impatient, this way may be less attractive than the direct struggle for immediate redress, but it is sure, it is within our power, it means the political education of the people, the winning of Liberty, the guarding of it when won. For Liberty is not safe under a statute, but under the spirit of the Nation. It may not win rapid redress of the Panjab atrocities, but it will make their repetition for ever impossible. It is the manly way of a virile Nation, conscious of its strength but also conscious of its present limitations, and it is the shortest road to HOME RULE.—*The Citizen.*

# NON-CO-OPERATION

By Annie Besant

The Non-Co-operation problem has entered a most peculiar phase: Non-Co-operation in principle and Co-operation in practice. The constant hammering of a handful of speakers and writers on the absurdity and impossibility of practising Non-Co-operation has had its effect on the public mind. The arguments have so filled the mental atmosphere that the advocates of Non-Co-operation use them unconsciously in favour of their contention that a general programme is impossible unless the collective wisdom of the National Congress can evolve something more acceptable than its constituent organisations can evolve. If a few dozen people cannot agree on a programme of action, there seems no likelihood that a few thousands will exhibit more uniformity—in fact, the probability is the other way. It seems likely that the Congress will pass an abstract academical resolution, accepting the principle of non-co-operation, and will pass a second resolution of the nature of the Amritsar compromise, which each man can interpret in his own way.

At the Madras Provincial Congress Committee a resolution was passed by a majority approving Non-Co-operation "in principle," but every resolution proposing a definite "programme," or fragments of a programme, was rejected. The Committee therefore approves the principle, but disapproves the practice—a singularly infructuous decision, which paralyses Non-Co-operative action instead of the Government. Non-Co-operation could not be practised in its entirety—that would be too inconvenient; everyone must draw the line somewhere. Mr. Gandhi drew *his* line at travelling by train, and so co-operated in making a large revenue for the Government; the speaker drew *his* line at boycotting the Councils; had he not the same right to draw lines as had Mr. Gandhi? There was no logic in politics. Another disapproved of boycotting the Courts; another of boycotting the schools and colleges. And so it went on. Finally, every programme resolution was boycotted, and the principle was left high and dry.

Thorough Non-Co-operation with the Government means that you set out to 'paralyse the Government', and therefore must not help or support it in any way. You must not go by train, use post or telegraph, hold any Government office paid or unpaid, seek redress at any court, register any document, accept protection from policeman or soldier, pay any tax. Other proposals are a social boycott of Government officers and of all Britons—even of those who co-operate with them—an industrial boycott of British goods, and so on. There are no lengths to which some people are not prepared to go (in words) to show their resentment and hatred. The real attraction of the movement is, I think, that it is a channel for resentment without entailing much loss or danger, unless you accept a programme. The really honest Non-Co-operators accept a definite programme and are prepared to carry it out. Most talk big and act little.

Is it legitimate to pass a resolution approving "the principle of Non-Co-operation"? No one who knows the history of Nations can deny that a Nation in bondage has a right to break its bonds, if the majority so wish. There is no right in one Nation to rule another which is unwilling to be so ruled; no right resides in the strength of a large Nation holding down a small one; a sword is not a legitimate sceptre. The right to revolt against a foreign yoke, or even against a home tyranny, has been asserted successfully in English, Scotch, French, Italian history, to say nothing of the American Revolution or the late war. No democrat can deny it. If a Government may, theoretically, under certain circumstances, be overthrown by force, so may it, theoretically, be overthrown by paralysis. An unarmed weak Nation, finding its Government intolerable, may wholly withdraw itself, leave the Government isolated, with nothing to govern and no power to administer. But just as it is silly to assert the right to make a Revolution and create a street riot, so it is silly to assert the empty right to Non-Co-operate, and have a few futile resignations. The Congress by passing such a resolution will only make the Nation ridiculous in the eyes of the world.

But it is important that everyone should understand that Non-Co-operation is a revolutionary method, as much as taking up arms. Attempts to transform Government by reforms are constitutional; to destroy a Government whether by machine-gun or paralysis is revolutionary, and to assert an empty right to kill by guns or by paralysis, when you can do neither, is childish. India should not lower herself in the eyes of the world by such empty assertions that she cannot carry out. Cannot? Yes, cannot, because her people are not sufficiently united nor sufficiently in earnest to make the sacrifices necessary to win freedom by a sudden leap. Mr. Montagu never spoke truer words than when he said: "When India is determined to have Home Rule, she will have it." Meanwhile, empty, useless resolutions are not consistent with her self-respect or her dignity.—*The Leader*.

---

[The following leading articles appeared in *New India* during May, June, July and August, 1920, and were nearly all written by Mrs. Annie Besant.]

## Mr. GANDHI AND NON-CO-OPERATION

We have reprinted Mr. Gandhi's very interesting article in *Young India*, on "How to Work Non-Co-operation" for it gives a gleam of hope that violence may be delayed, and by delay may become impracticable, ere the danger point is reached. Mr. Gandhi remarks that the stages are not simultaneous but progressive, and one must be a failure before the next is attempted:

> The first is the giving up of titles and resignation of honorary posts. If there is no response or if the response received is not effective, recourse will be had to the second stage. The second stage involves much previous arrangement. Certainly not a single servant will be called out unless he is either capable of supporting himself and his dependents or the Khilafat Committee is able to bear the burden.

The first will be an interesting experiment, for it will test the reality of the feeling behind the movement. No harm will be done by it to anyone, and it will in the way trouble the Government; the holders of titles will lose the pleasure of having them, but the loss will not be of a serious character and will be more than made up for by the applause which will greet it. It will diminish the supply of candidates for the new Councils from the "Nationalist" ranks, from which we may expect all the Non-Co-operators to come, and this will smooth the paths of the Liberals, the Home Rulers, and the Wreckers.

The second stage, it is admitted, we are glad to see, demands "much previous arrangement". Mr. Gandhi recognises the fact that provision must be made for their maintenance before the Government servants are called on to resign their livelihood. Under the circumstances, the carrying out of the second step cannot be made for a considerable time. If the response be not general, so as to paralyse Government administration, we may take it for granted that the failure of the policy will be accepted, and Non-Co-operation will be stopped. It can only succeed if huge numbers carry it out, and if only a few sacrifice themselves, no effective pressure on Government can result. Mr. Gandhi writes as to this:

> The second stage must be entirely successful, if the response is at all on an adequate scale. For no Government—much less the Indian Government—can subsist if the people cease to serve it. The withdrawal therefore of the police and the military—the third stage—is a distant goal. The organisers however wanted to be fair, open and above suspicion. They did not want to keep back from the Government or the public a single step they had in contemplation even as a remote contingency.

But suppose the response is inadequate, unsatisfactory and disappointing, what then? Mr. Gandhi is playing for a huge stake; can he win it? Can he afford to lose it? It is certain that no Government can exist, if the people decline to serve, but suppose they do not resign on a sufficiently large scale? Then the weapon is broken in the hand. No analogous movement has over been successful without pressure being put on those who did not wish to join, and such pressure has constantly been used in strikes, in boycotts and the rest. When people are suffering from having given up their work, it is maddening to see others at work, and to know that their work means failure of one's own pressure on the opposing force. One's own comrades become one's enemies, enemies that are making impossible the success of the cause for which one is suffering, and resentment soon bursts out into violence.

The third step "is a distant goal," and if Mr. Gandhi and Moulana Shaukat Ali can hold their people in from violence during the second period, the third may never arise. Complete success or complete failure would put an end to the movement; what is most to be feared is an indeterminate result, which might encourage the Non-Co-operators to go on to the third step, which would mean civil anarchy. We may leave the "suspension of taxes" aside, as that "is still more remote," and in fact cannot arise, for if the Government survive the third step there will be no refusal to pay taxes, while if the people survive there will be no Government to levy them.

On the whole, we have probably three or four months of breathing time before the outbreak of the storm. The electricity may disperse itself before the time comes for action, for popular enthusiasm is a very fleeting thing. Some other excitement may attract them before the time is ripe, and the visit of the Prince of Wales may prove more attractive than the struggle for the Khalifa. A rumour has risen as to the Amir of Afghanistan as Khalifa. The Arabs may put forward a candidate. There are many possibilities that may arise if time permit. A crowd may be stimulated by religious enthusiasm to rush on machine-guns. But to stand quietly with folded arms demands a higher quality than is as yet possessed by a normal crowd.

---

## NON-CO-OPERATION

MR. GANDHI forces us back to fundamentals, and in that he does the Indian Nation a great service. There are words that catch the fancy, that sound innocuous, or as implying but a little risk; that suggest a plan so effective, so easy to carry out, if only everyone will play his part in the drama, and the dénouement is so splendid. A whole Nation united as one; Hindu and Muslim standing shoulder to shoulder as brothers; 315 millions of people of one heart and one mind. What Government can resist their demand? What Government would be mad enough to try? And how little it is that is asked of the Nation; just to sit still with folded arms. To do nothing. Merely not to co-operate with the Government. Could any struggle be more simple, yet more effective? No anger, no violence. The triumph of moral, of spiritual force in defence of a righteous cause. Mr. Gandhi leads the movement; all is well.

Some of us, however, looking into the simple procedure suggested, see in it possibilities of danger, probability of violence, either a failure because only a few obey the call, or a triumph ending in anarchy. Mr. Gandhi admits the risk, but says that not to offer a channel by which the deep resentment may flow away is more dangerous than to open the channel to the current. If the Government does not yield, the responsibility is on the Government. That the Indian Government is as helpless as he is to change the decisions of the Supreme Council of the Allies does not seem to affect him. He is always convinced that his view is the right view, and that those who do not agree with him are suffering from a defect in their moral vision; if harm comes of his view and his method of enforcing it, the responsibility is not his.

Argument being futile, one betakes oneself to the careful consideration of his project. One comes to the conclusion that step No. 1 does not matter, and is even useful as a test of sincerity. Such tremendous promises of devotion to death have been pledged; such tremendous assertions that 315 millions of people are behind the demand have been made; that one willingly awaits the beginning of the proof by comparatively easy performances. Step No. 2 means, if successful, the paralysing of the Government administration, a collapse of the civil Government, in fact. If it succeeds, Government ceases to exist. One need hardly go further. We should never reach step No. 3. There would be no posts, no telegraphs, little transport, no courts, the whole machinery would be stopped. How this would affect the Supreme Council or the Khalifa, no one explains. How it would affect India, who is in no wise to blame, is obvious.

A result so tremendous gives us furiously to think. If Non-Co operation with Government means this, to begin with, what is the real fact as to Co-operation? We begin to realise that Co-operation between the people and the Government is the very basis of Society, and that without it, Society ceases to exist, and is reduced to a mob of individuals; law disappears, order vanishes, the strongest rules, anarchy prevails. Out of barbarism man has risen by Co-operaiton; into barbarism he returns if he adopts Non-Co-operation. We realise that this innocent seeming phrase, "Non-Co-operation with Government," is really a declaration of war against Society; it is no moral nor spiritual force, but an appeal to physical force which strikes at the very basis of Society and of civilised life.

We see that where one man pits his conscience against the law of his day, he appeals really to a moral and spiritual force; he suffers but he does not rend in twain the social bonds; these continue though he may die; his sufferings appeal; they touch the heart; they arouse the mind; if he be inspired by God and is striking a really higher note, he, or his successors, conquer and Society is lifted higher. But if thousands of men follow this same course, they conquer by numbers not by suffering; they terrify Government into submission by the physical force of their numbers, not by a moral or spiritual appeal. The one is a martyr; the thousands are revolutionaries; the passive resistance of the one becomes the shattering force of the thousands who make Government impossible by refusing the Co-operation on which Society is based.

Revolution may sometimes be justifiable, may be inevitable, may be brought about by intolerable suffering, by intolerable oppression. All we desire to press here is that the refusal of Co-operation is a deliberate paralysing of Government, and that it ought only to be suggested with the same calculation of forces, the same balancing of resources, the same recognition of responsibility, as the decision to make a revolution. It is not a matter for wild excitement and frenzied platform exhortation, but one for a council of war and the perfecting of a civil and military organisation.

Those who are not prepared for this tremendous responsibility had better not indulge in this camouflage of words, but try to realise what they are doing and asking others to do. They are undermining the very basis of Society with singular light-heartedness and irresponsibility. The first step is already taken by a few. Let all at least think, before they take the second.

---

## NON-CO-OPERATION AND EXPEDIENCY

The Editor of the *Independent* published on June 1st a reasoned leader regarding Non-Co-operation. Upon this subject, any pronouncement which does not emanate from politicians whose self-interest is known to outweigh their principles warrants careful consideration in view of the immense importance of the principle and practice at stake. We therefore make no apology for scrutinising in detail Mr. Bipin Chandra Pal's discussion.

He first declares that with India situated as she is, the Non-Co-operation policy is the last weapon of extremity; next, that there is an ethical obligation to refuse to accept any wrong without an effort to end it. Since Non-Co-operation is to be used when a Government is despotic or bureaucratic, its ethical value becomes absolute, and no question of expediency can arise, as the Non-Co-operators withdraw from the Government for conscientious reasons.

The writer justifies the conscience of the Musalmans, saying that the matter must be left to the

> decision of the Muhammadans themselves. No non-Muhammadan can or ought to say anything in this matter until the Muhammadans have themselves decided what they should do one way or the other. It is only after our Muhammadan brethren have come to a definite decision on the subject that our own turn will come to decide whether and how far we can or ought to co-operate with them in this matter.

After this, non-Musalmans, though not approaching the question from the standpoint of individual conscience, are to make up their minds in the matter on the political, since they have no conscientious, grounds. Mr. Pal then proceeds to state that the first question will be: Is there any chance of success in a movement of this kind? Only after this preliminary question has been settled, will it be the duty of the leaders to consider other and more serious questions in regard to it.

This argument leads one to suppose that the *Independent* has very serious doubts about the successful working of the Non-Co-operation scheme. Its hope that the Khilafat Conference will "consider with all seriousness" strengthens our view of the *Independent's* attitude. But whether this is so or not, we are very far from agreeing with the *Independent* that the first question is to determine whether or not the movement will succeed. For success, if it calls out the utmost extremities of the movement, means the disruption of the National life; and failure means the disrepute of a great public movement; so that whatever eventuates, the Non-Co-operation proposal endangers the State.

The leader we are quoting then winds up with this paragraph:

> As regards ourselves, we frankly confess that the seriousness and complexity of the question stagger us. And realising all this, we cannot rush with the self-confidence of some of our Moderate contemporaries to commit ourselves off-hand and without watching further development, one way or the other, on this question.

We do not know who are the Moderate contemporaries referred to, or whether anybody in this country whose views are worth the least consideration has done any "committing off-hand". What has been done in some quarters, ourselves amongst others, was to help to give the country a lead in this matter because of the extreme danger involved in it, both to political and physical life. It is absolutely vital that no one in a responsible position should burke his duty of expressing views on momentous matters like this, and if in spite of the Khilafat Conference's decision, the forthcoming Calcutta Special Congress comes to see wisdom with regard to the dangerous proposal, it will be due to those contemporaries of the *Independent* who courageously faced the rising tide of public opinion and expressed the truth as it appeared, and still appears, to them. When a section of the country opposed the first Satyāgraha movement on the ground that there was nothing left passively to resist, and persistently refused to break other laws than that one particularly aimed at, it had to endure a terrible storm of public reproach, though it cannot be denied that that section was in a large degree absolutely right. It is to their credit that they have now, in spite of the present high feeling, again taken a stand against this more serious form of Non-Co-operation, intended to bring pressure upon and finally entirely disorganise the Government and to obstruct the Secretary of State, who have done everything they possibly could to press a solution of the Turkish problem with fairness in the matter of the Khilafat.

There is a great deal of very woolly thinking just now in our public life, and the high feelings which have been aroused over the Hunter Committee Report tend to create a mass of emotions which entirely distort our mental outlook. Though this may not be the case with the *Independent*, it is certainly true of many sections of the country; and it is therefore incumbent upon the *Independent* to be all the more clear and full in the expression of its views. It is not very helpful to descend upon Moderates who are doing what they can to think calmly, and to help the country also to see its way in a rational manner.

---

## NON-CO-OPERATION POSSIBILITIES

It is impossible to conceive of any legitimate reason for professed leaders of political opinion in this country refraining from expressing their views in this matter of non-co-operation. Devotees of those who advocate "diplomacy" and "policy" may be satisfied with the silence of their chosen leaders in this matter. We are acquainted with the absurd suggestion that the business of a leader is to find out what the country is going to do before he commits himself, but even that extraordinary idea of leadership does not cover the case of a politician who advocates Non-Co-operation where it is convenient for him to do so, and ignores the issue otherwise.

There are certain limited sequential possibilities in respect to Non-Co-operation in its practical aspects in reference to the Khilafat. The Committee which Mr. Gandhi leads is now bound to start action shortly. Putting aside for a moment the progressive steps, let us consider the degrees in which response may be given to the call to action, and the inevitable results of each such measure of response.

In the first place, the minimum result of the Committee's call is that Mr. Gandhi will be followed by a few educated Muhammadans, a very small number of genuine Satyāgrahis, and a fermenting dash of don't-care Immoderate politicians. It is improbable that this comparatively small group, getting only such a small response in the country, will proceed to try to rouse the uneducated classes of Musalmans; and it will certainly not attempt to stir the bulk of the Hindus. This eventuality thus merely means a colossal fiasco.

If, however, the educated Muhammadans stand together in very large numbers or as a whole, accompanied as before by some genuine Satyāgrahis attracted by Mr. Gandhi, and the aforesaid yeast of don't-care Immoderates, it is bound to take with it the much less intelligent and less controlled feelings of great groups of Musalmans here and there in India, probably mostly in the North, whose outbursts of feeling will certainly be tinged with fanaticism in some few places. It is useless to deny that this will lead to a certain amount of violence, for even if the Police and Army in India contain no more than feeble imitation-Dyers—which the most optimistic will not expect—the mere maintenance of order is bound to produce fire somewhere, and that fire conflagration. Even granting for the moment the quite impossible hope of a peaceful movement, the resignation of Muhammadans from their posts will mean the coming in of Hindus (as we have already seen in Madras), and the resentment which the educated Muhammadans will thus have intensified is sure to communicate itself to other classes.

The third possibility, stellar in its remoteness, is that at the word, Hindu and Musalman, as one man, the country will rise behind Mr. Gandhi—and equally as one man will sit down again with the perfect resignation of the Satyāgrahi and only passively resist. We cannot picture this as an actual outcome. In the first place, the bonds between Hindus and Musalmans are not such as will enable the two communities to work under the strain which is bound to be put upon them. In the second place, the campaign of education which must necessarily precede Non-Co-operation, if it is also to result in non-violence, has not been accomplished among the Hindus, and is infinitely further from having been accomplished amongst Musalmans. Even if the whole country acts unitedly in the matter, we are then face to face with what will be the real failure of Non-Co-operation, namely, the paralysis through the progressive steps of a Government which has done all it could to meet the needs of Islam.

With this eventuality we have dealt at length previously, and our views are well-known. It is further more increasingly the view of the whole country. Our concern here and now is with those people who claim to voice public opinion, especially public opinion in the South of India who, through their chosen medium, *The Hindu* and its Editor, do not face this issue. Where there is any escape from the logical lines we have laid down is entirely beyond our understanding. If *The Hindu* would present factors with which we are unacquainted, we would be greatly obliged. Until it does so, what trust can be placed in it? Either a man really believes in Non-Co-operation, or he does not. If he does, it seems to us his duty is to educate the country in the matter of Non-Co-operation, to make sure that it will be non-violent, and ceaselessly to press it forward. The Editor of *The Hindu* does believe in it, for he has personally given his support to it. Why does he not stand by his belief, and help to save the country from the violence which many believe will result from its practice?

---

## NON-CO-OPERATION

THE question of the application of Non-Co-Operation as a remedy for grievances seems to be widening out. The new autocratic government of India has issued its first ukase, stating that they "expect every one to respond to their recommendation," and informing us that "those who realise their responsibility and the gravity of the cause will not act independently," as success "is dependent upon strict obedience to instructions". We certainly do not realise any responsibility to this self-appointed dictator and his committee, but of the gravity of the situation he is provoking none can have any doubt.

We are now given the programme of part of the first step in Non-Co-operation, and there are eight duties imposed on the Nation:

(1) Surrender of all titles of honour and honorary offices.

(2) Non-participation in Government loans.

(3) Suspension by lawyers of practice and settlement of civil disputes by private arbitration.

(4) Boycott of Government schools by parents.

(5) Boycott of the Reformed Councils.

(6) Non-participation in Government parties, and such other functions.

(7) Refusal to accept any civil or military post in Mesopotamia, or to offer as Units for the army, especially for service in the Turkish territories now being administered in violation of pledges.

PROPAGATE SWADESHI

(8) Vigorous prosecution of "Swadeshi" inducing the people, at the time of this national and religious awakening, to appreciate their primary duty to their country, by being satisfied with its own productions and manufactures.

No. 1 has long been with us. No. 2 is a new departure presumably suggested by the new loan. No. 3 is interesting as a test of the sincerity of the many Vakils who have enthusiastically proclaimed their adherence to Non-Co-operation. Will the Courts be emptied on August 1, and the fees returned for the breach of contract? Then comes a fresh idea; the children are to be withdrawn from Government schools, a new application of the visiting of the sins of the fathers on the children. Lala Lajpat Rai has supplied No. 5, the boycotting of the new Councils. That is a good hearing for the Liberals, as the Non-Co-operators are neo-Nationalists. "No Government parties" is the stern command of No. 6. Large numbers of people boycotted Government functions in Bengal after the Partition, but "nobody seemed one penny the worse". No. 7 bars acceptance of any civil or military post in Mesopotamia or enlisting in the Army, and No. 8 is the "vigorous prosecution of Swadeshi". It is to be hoped that following Swadeshi, carried out by many of us before Mr. Gandhi's late insistence on it, does not forbid the wearing of the exquisite fabrics for which India has been famous from time immemorial, and the donning of the very unsightly cloth dear to Mr. Gandhi's heart.

Another most mischievous item has been added to this long list, but not by the Council of Autocracy. The Ahmedabad Branch of the "Home Rule League for India," presumably the League of which Mr. Gandhi is President, though the name is new, finds that it will be its "painful duty" "to advise people not to join any movement that may be started to welcome H. R. H. the Prince of Wales," unless His Majesty's Government obeys the demand to:

1. Repeal the Rowlatt Act,
2. Recall the Viceroy,
3. Impeach Sir Michael O'Dwyer,
4. Publicly try General Dyer, Col. Johnson, Col. O'Brien, Mr. Bosworth Smith, Rai Saheb Shrī Ram Sud and Malik Saheb Khan, and

5. Give statutory guarantees for the non-repetition of the various atrocities perpetrated under the Martial Law régime.

It would be difficult to discover a more irrational demand than this. What has the Prince of Wales to do with these matters? How can he influence the performance of any one of them? The Prince is the representative of the King-Emperor, who is a constitutional Monarch, compelled to accept the decisions of his Parliament, his Ministers. He has no more power to impeach Sir Michael O'Dwyer, than has a member of this Branch of one of the Home Rule Leagues. The proposal to offer a gross insult to the Nation's guest, to stain India's reputation even for hospitality, is a scandalous one, so long as India is part of the Empire, for gross rudeness to the Crown it acknowledges has never been India's way.

It would be interesting to know what statutory guarantees would suffice to prevent the repetition of the Martial Law atrocities. When Martial Law is proclaimed, ordinary statutes give no protection. As this request cannot be granted, we fear the Ahmedabad Branch will have to perform its "painful duty".

It is evident that we are going from bad to worse, becoming more and more extravagant and ridiculous under Mr. Gandhi's leadership. The responsibility for this must rest on the shoulders of the Congress leaders, who have not the courage to stand up against him and warn the Nation of the dangers into which he is leading it. They all treat him with such reverence as a Saint, a "Mahatma," a spiritual leader, that the crowd naturally looks up to and obeys him, and they have not the courage to say that this new scheme is a hundredfold more dangerous than his law-breaking campaign of last year. It is the people, the helpless, loving, trusting, obedient, people who will be the victims, and when he fails, as he failed over the effort to repeal the Rowlatt Act, it is they who will suffer from the triumph of the reactionaries, rendered inevitable by the policy he is seeking to impose. His work will be pointed to as the justification of bureaucracy, as the proof that the Sydenhams and the O'Dwyers were right.

# NON-CO-OPERATION

THE fateful 1st of August has come and gone, and we are not much more advanced in our knowledge of the views of the Nation on Mr. Gandhi's fourfold scheme, than we were before it dawned on us. The passing away of Bala Gangadhar Tilak somewhat overshadowed the hartal, as many closed their shops on that account, irrespective of Mr. Gandhi's behest. He himself sent to the Viceroy his Kaiser-i-Hind and War Medals, with the statement that he no longer felt either respect or affection for the Government. Mrs. Sarala Devi Choudhrani returned her War Brooch with an explanatory letter, and an Honorary Magistrate resigned his office at Guntur. The Madras Khilafat Committee announced that it would declare resignations later—a proceeding which does not suggest a large stream of resignations. But it is early times, and in a few days, the trickle may have swollen into a torrent.

I am concerned more with the principle underlying the movement than with its immediate success or failure, for I do not think that many people recognise the closeness of the web into which people and Government are interwoven, so that the paralysis of the Government, which is Mr. Gandhi's avowed aim, would mean the dislocation of the National life. It is for the purpose of bringing this home to the people, that I have made the suggestion that the Government should take part in the game of Non-Co-operation, not with police and soldiers, but by the withdrawal of all Government services from leading non-co-operators, by a good-humoured acquiescence in their proposal, and by non-co-operating with them. Such action would paralyse their movement very much more rapidly than they can paralyse the Government. And the effective carrying out of the idea would not be difficult.

I do not suggest that the Government should trouble itself with the small folk of the movement, but only with the leaders. The ruling Committee is in Bombay, and from Bombay come all the orders. If no letters, no telegrams were delivered to or from that guiding Committee, and if all Khilafat Committees were similarly isolated; if the leading newspapers advocating Non-Co-operation were equally non-co-operated with by any Government agency; if, so far as they are known, no tickets were issued to Non-Co-operators at any railway station, and their messengers were left to private motors, carriages and bullock carts, the difficulties of effectively carrying on their organisation would be insuperable, and they would learn how much they are dependent upon Government in their everyday life. They would find themselves continually knocking up against barriers, and reduced to a simplicity of life which may be ideally attractive, but would be practically most inconvenient. I am afraid that Governments are too conventional and too wedded to precedent to adopt such an easy method, decorated with so little red tape, and they will prefer their cumbrous methods, sanctified by custom.

*The Pioneer* wants to know whether I—no, I beg its pardon, why " an Indian Nationalist paper " belonging to the " advanced Indian Home Rulers," but regarding Non-Co-operation " with marked disfavour "—" in putting forward this suggestion, it "—the said paper—had fully thought out all the consequences that the adoption of such a policy would imply ". I do not suppose I have thought of all of them, but I have thought of a good many, including all *The Pioneer*—no, an Anglo-Indian Allahabad contemporary—has suggested and more. I have imagined newspapers confined to local news; lying in bags that no mail will carry away; persons assaulted or robbed whom no policeman will help; suitors to whom no Judge will listen; deeds which no Registrar will stamp; wills which no executor can prove—the disabilities are endless. *The Pioneer* thinks that " there is a good deal to be said for this suggestion," and that " our contemporary's suggestion might be worth consideration ".

It does not seem to have quite grasped the objection to " executive orders touching liberty and property," and my preference for the use of the Criminal Code. Yet it is surely an elementary right in the eyes of an Englishman, that his liberty and property should only be taken away from him after open trial and sentence of a Court of Law, and not by the whim of an Executive. That is all I ask for. It says, quite truly, that if people riot the Government must intervene and stop the rioting. Granted. The only question is what to do with the rioter *after* arresting him. Shall he be locked up without charge and without trial for an indefinite term at a Governor's pleasure, or shall he be charged, and then tried before one of His Majesty's Judges, and if found guilty be sentenced? Further, if a man be arrested who is not a rioter, is he to be dealt with by Executive order, or a Court of Law? I claim an open trial and not a *lettre de cachet*. The one is to live under an autocracy; the other is to live under law.

I wonder if any Government will be wise enough to checkmate Non-Co-operation by Non-Co-operation. It would win, "hands down".

---

## NON-CO-OPERATION

THE visit of Mr. Gandhi to Madras will see a noteworthy readjustment of parties divided on the question of Non-Co-operation. Liberals, National Home Rule Leaguers, and people of Mr. S. Srinivasa Iyengar's way of thinking, are strongly against the policy of withdrawing Co-operation from Government. Mr. Iyengar has indeed gone so far as to express a string of Liberal opinions which should have appeared as gall and wormwood to his followers. Mr. Gandhi's movement was, he has said emphatically, unconstitutional; it was not practicable to such an extent as to conform to the demands of Indians, and the time had not arrived for such a movement. There is a remarkable likeness in the views expressed recently by Mrs. Besant and Mr. Iyengar. The former has written in the last issue of *The Citizen*:

> What then is the way out? I fear there is only one sure way, for even resolutions, protests, meetings, will soon be overborne by the pressing interest of the elections. None the less, they should not be despised, for all we have gained so far has been the result of these now-contemned methods of constitutional agitation, and even now the Central Government is being pushed by it into action, inadequate though that action be. There is only one way, because others are barred. Revolution by violence is inexpedient and impossible. Revolution by non-violence, non-co-operation, leads either to anarchy or futility. What is left? Working to get our very best men into the Councils . . . etc.

Mr. Iyengar told the Provincial Congress Committee the other day, that the limits of constitutional agitation had not been reached. He said:

> He did not agree with those who thought that constitutional agitation was altogether useless now. What they had got up till

now was only by constitutional agitation. The Reform Act might be good or bad. But did they get it by non-co-operation? Did they get the Executive Council Membership by non-co-operation? He therefore thought non-co-operation with the Government in its entirety was thoroughly unconstitutional, and if any step was followed as a means to that end, it was equally unconstitutional.

Mr. Gandhi is very explicit on this question: he has stated that he owes no allegiance to the Government and that the movement he has started is intended to paralyse the Government. A policy which, in its result, will make the existence of Government impossible cannot but be unconstitutional, especially after its founder has explained the motives actuating him in starting it.

So far as the apostles of Non-Co-Operation and its opponents are concerned, the matter is quite simple. Support or no support from the Congress, Mr. Gandhi is determined to pursue his course and he states the case for following his conscience in the latest issue of *Young India* with his usual simplicity and candour. The mandate of the Special Congress, should it decline to resolve upon Non-Co-operation, will not bind him; in a similar way, it will not bind others who are conscientiously against it. But the question is: What becomes of that very large class of people who have all along been thinking, in spite of asseverations to the contrary, that the movement was constitutional, and that they would be perfectly within due bounds by following Mr. Gandhi? Many of them, it is true, have been under the belief that Non-Co-operation was mere bluff, and that the time would never come for their putting it into practice. And, if it came to the pinch, they would back out of the movement without so much as a verbal regret. But the position of some others is different. They have proclaimed from the house-tops that Non-Co-operation was the only remedy for the ills that India was suffering from at present. The trouble in the case of these Nationalists is Mr. Gandhi—his "tyranny," as it has been termed, his acid tests. Two courses are possible for them. They may disagree with Mr. Gandhi in his characterisation of the movement (see *Young India* of 28th July) as tending to put the very existence of Government into jeopardy, but say it is perfectly constitutional and support Mr. Gandhi. This, of course, will be the manly course to take, but it may be safely predicted that the bulk of them will not do so. They would rather have recourse to the other alternative, now that things are taking a serious shape, of disowning Mr. Gandhi, and telling him: "Look here, Mr. Gandhi: you say that the object of Non-Co-operation is to end the Government and you have made statements about your want of loyalty, etc., with which we cannot agree. If such be the motives that inspire you, we cannot co-operate with you." Such a line of retreat, especially when all the implications of Non-Co-operation have been from the beginning before the public, will be that of the combatant-swaggerer who was not prepared for a serious encounter. But there is no other way of escape from the *impasse*.

There is another little difficulty created by the mandate theory. The resolutions of the Tinnevelly Conference may not have the same weight as those of the Congress and so they may be disregarded with impunity. But the decisions of the Congress must be binding upon its adherents; otherwise they will not be Congressmen. Mr. Gandhi, of all exponents of Non-Co-operation, is the only leader who has stated that he would go on, whatever the Special Congress may say. But Lala Lajpat Rai, Pandit Malaviyaji and the lesser lights in our own Province have clearly urged on their countrymen to wait and follow the lead of the Congress. One of the Nationalist newspapers wrote recently as follows:

> The All-India Muslim League and the Special Congress have to meet and consider and come to a final decision for the whole country on the question of non-co-operation, including its details. However, valuable the opinions of eminent leaders may be, the fact must not be lost sight of that the National Congress is the great national organisation whose decision will be accepted as binding on the country.

There is already a flutter in the Nationalist dove-cotes. The cry is being raised that if the Gandhi policy of Non-Co-operation is adopted by the Congress, then it would not necessarily bind all people, because it is a thing of religion, it is not a matter of mere voting, it is *Paramarthika vishayam*, and so on. Leading Nationalists, dreading the prospect of being dethroned, are passionately pleading for its being kept as a non-party programme. We shall not be surprised if these pathetic appeals are listened to, and Nationalist leaders who are unable to follow Mr. Gandhi—supposing that the Special Congress approves of that programme—are released by the Party from the obligation to follow the Mandate. That would only be consistent with their whole policy, never consistent or understandable. With a view to avoid this contingency, some ingenious minds are also already planning other, certainly innocent and perfectly innocuous, methods of Non-Co-operation, such as refusing to co-operate with Liberals, and so on !

---

## RESPONSIBILITY ?

THE Hijrat movement to Afghanistan is proving to be the failure that all outsiders expected. Afghanistan is a poor country, and the sudden entrance of several thousand almost impecunious people has proved to be too great a strain on its resources. The Amir enlisted some Indians who were willing to join his army, and these he declines to set free ; a number of others who are unable to support themselves he has turned back and he has peremptorily refused to admit any more. The practicable roads into Afghanistan are not many ; they are congested by the Mahajirins, and the ordinary caravans necessary to Afghanistan cannot get through. Returning Mahajirins are furious with those who induced them to emigrate without making arrangements for their welfare, and those who sold off their lands, many at low prices, are desperate. The bureaucracy is therefore appealed to for succour, and the Government officials are trying to find means to settle them again on their old lands. We appeal to Moulana Shaukat Ali and the Khilafat Committees, who have led these poor co-religionists of theirs to this will-o'-the-wisp of Hijrat, to use the funds they have raised to buy back the lands sold under their impulse, and thus to make good, to some small extent, the misery they have caused. It is sufficient humiliation to have to appeal for help to the Government with which they refuse to co-operate, but perhaps they may thus learn the salutary lesson of Co-operation.

Men who stir up the masses to action, and have not the insight to place before them a safe goal, nor the courage to oppose them when they are inclined to go headlong, have no right to lead. Perhaps they may understand now why I, having taken a leading part in stirring up the masses to accept the Idéal of Home Rule—the noblest Ideal—have faced unpopularity, when the road to it was opened by the Reform Act, in order to induce them to tread that road and not to erect barricades of obstruction on it, or to rush headlong along a path leading inevitably to revolution. Every popular leader must shoulder responsibility for the movement he makes or helps, and be ready to face unpopularity and abuse when people without insight continue to impel when the moment calls for control. If the Congress endorses the policy of Non-Co-operation against the Reform Act and the Rules, it enters on the path of revolution. Every man who realises the nature of the crisis and is against revolution should attend the Calcutta Congress. For *there* is the fateful decision to be taken. The All-India Congress Committee decided to call a Special Congress and to place in its hands the decision as to whether Non-Co-operation should be used : (1) In support of the Muslims; (2) to obtain redress for the Panjab atrocities; (3) as a protest against the inadequacy of the Reform Act and the Rules. These are the issues to be decided. None can deny their gravity. Whatever there is of insight, courage, and self-sacrifice among Indian political leaders should compel their presence in this Valley of Decision.

Fortunately there has been time for the Moderates, the Liberals and the National Home Rulers largely to change the current of public opinion on the Reform Act; those who talked loudly in favour of the "No, thank you," policy at Amritsar, those who denounced it as "the shadow of a shade," those who proclaimed that only by wrecking the Act could a better one be gained, those who abused Mr. Montagu and who called those who refused to follow the Amritsar policy rebels and traitors, Rākshasas and dogs, have now modified their policy, and accept the Moderate axiom to co-operate with the Government where possible and oppose it where necessary. They have followed the Liberal and National Home Rule lead, while continuing to abuse them, in the hope of covering their retreat. They will condemn their old policy and endorse ours when they oppose at Calcutta the use of Non-Co-operation as a protest against the Reform Act and the Rules. If they even accept it as a principle, they cannot enter the Councils—unless for pure unmitigated obstruction—for there they must co-operate with the Government in passing useful legislation; they cannot be Councillors nor Ministers, for that means entering the Government itself. Now that Great Britain has accepted our Home Rule Ideal we have every reason to co-operate with the Government in every way that increases and widens the Reforms, for as Mr. Montagu pointed out twice in the Joint Committee, there is nothing in the Act to prevent the reserved subjects being transferred, or to prevent a liberal Governor from treating all reserved subjects as transferred, even without formal transfer. Thus we can reach full Provincial Autonomy under this "inadequate, unsatisfactory and disappointing" Act, and immediately win our provincial ideal by Reform instead of by Revolution. As regards the Central Government, we have at least two Home Rulers, Messrs. Sapru and Sarma, in the Executive Council, and may have some in the Council of State and the Legislative Assembly.

We, who raised the standard of Home Rule as necessary to National self-respect, have therefore nothing to regret in the bold departure we took. We made the advance possible and those of us who shouldered the responsibility of crying "Halt," when the crowd wanted to rush, did our clear duty to the movement. Let us now in the Congress as in local Conferences, in press and on platform, face this revolutionary Non-Co-operation, and continue to work for our Ideal along the pathway of Reform.

---

## N.-C.-O. WHAT WILL IT DO?

We have not heard that, as a result of Mr. Gandhi's advice to the huge gathering on the Beach on Thursday to boycott schools and colleges and law courts, there has been any diminution in attendance at any of these institutions. Until we hear to the contrary, we shall continue to hold that for all the repetition of his arguments as to the constitutional nature of his "beautiful and unanswerable" method of Non-Co-operation, or its wonderful efficacy, parents will still continue to send their children to the institutions maintained or supported by the Government; lawyers will still prefer to assist in the distribution of British-made justice to producing "home-made and Swadeshi" justice through arbitration courts. The truth is, Mr. Gandhi errs lamentably in believing in the press-the-button-in-India device for solving National and International questions in Europe. We do not believe an Imperial Government like that of the British Empire is so perfectly conceived a piece of machinery that pressure in any part will be felt by the whole, and produce the desired result. And in any case, it is extremely doubtful whether Mr. Gandhi can wield the necessary force, or give it the necessary direction, to reduce the Government to paralysis. He claims to have weaned Mr. Shaukat Ali from violence. But we would respectfully remind Mr. Gandhi that the movement contains others besides this great Musalman leader, and that even his convert claims to reserve the right to violence. If the movement should go wrong and burst into violence, his public career, he declares, will come to an immediate termination. His retirement to the forest will help us little, we may be permitted to state, in the confusion and rioting that many justly apprehend. He claims that Mr. Montagu's successors will give him credit for having started this movement just as Mr. Montagu has praised his past services. It is not our ambition to attempt to be prophetic, because the present is pregnant enough with painful possibilities to absorb all our thoughts. One thing Mr. Gandhi made clear, if indeed such clarity were at all necessary. Whatever the decision of the Special Congress may be, he will pursue his propaganda of Non-Co-operation. It is intelligible that on questions of conscience and of moral obligation, a political body of whatever eminence cannot be the final judge. Mr. Gandhi is too shrewd a man, besides, not to see that the size of his audiences is not a measure of the size of his following. The verdict of the Special Congress, if the Nationalists have their way, will be in favour of "Non-Co-operation of some sort," probably of boycott of British goods. So far, except in one or two instances, no one has come forward to boycott Councils. Those that have not done so are presumably assisting an immoral Government to continue its wicked ways and are, therefore, themselves tainted. Does it not follow, that the children of lawyers must leave their parental roofs? Mr. Gandhi put forward the view, in a recent issue of *Young India*, that where a father acts unjustly it is the duty of the children to leave his protection. Similarly, if one section or sections of the community refuse to Non-Co-operate, is it not the duty of other brother-communities that are convinced of the immorality of the Government to extend the same treatment to them? Where does Mr. Gandhi draw the line, or does he draw the line at all? In the one case, he is holding an untenable position; in the other, he is advocating an utter dissolution of Society, to which the world even in its most primitive stage cannot hold a parallel. There is not the slightest reference, we observe, to the Rowlatt Act, a measure to which Mr. Gandhi objected on conscientious grounds as vehemently as he does to the Khilafat wrong, to which, on Lala Lajpat Rai's suggestion, has since been added the Panjab. Can conscientious objections lie dormant or be awakened at the instance of friends? We must recall the fact that after the Panjab disturbances of last year, the entire attention of the country was diverted to a demand for justice against the wrong-doers. The Rowlatt Act, it has almost been forgotten, continues to disgrace the Statute Book. But agitation against it has died down completely, for the sole reason that the remedy which Mr. Gandhi proposed and applied, in spite of grave warnings, being worse than the disease itself, public opinion has been busy since with all the direct and indirect developments of civil disobedience. The Panjab and Khilafat wrongs still cry aloud for justice. Non-Co-operation is already diverting public attention from these to itself. It may, or may not, as we earnestly hope, lead to violence. But it will most certainly not lead to the results which Mr. Gandhi contemplates.

---

## NON-CO-OPERATION

By Annie Besant

[Mrs. Annie Besant has contributed the following special article to the Congress Number of the *Looker On*. Mrs. Besant, whom many hold to be the greatest influence for good in India, admittedly the most capable of her sex now living, a power in politics whose strength is not yet realised by her opponents, writes as she speaks—eloquently, fearlessly, convincingly and crystal-clearly.—Editor.]

I believe that Mr. Gandhi's proposal of Non-Co-operation with the Government, with his fourfold programme of successive stages, and his hope thereby to paralyse the Government and thus to compel its submission to his view of its duty, is wrong in principle and will be disastrous to the country in proportion as it is carried out.

In principle, it is (i) revolutionary: Mr. Gandhi proposes to "paralyse" the Government, to render it powerless, unable to govern. The fact that he does not propose to kill its members does not alter the fact that he is striving to bring about a Revolution, for, whether you kill the Government with machine-guns or by paralysis, the end is the same. You overthrow the Government. At first, Mr. Gandhi proposed to substitute nothing in its stead; now he goes a step further, and says that the people should go to their own courts, form their own police for preserving order, and, presumably, pay taxes to support them.

(ii) Non-Co-operation stirs up hatred between Government and people, setting the people against the Government, which Mr. Gandhi describes as wicked and cruel. In addition to this, it stirs up race-hatred. Its popularity is due to the fact that large numbers of Indians feel bitter resentment against the Government on account of the Panjab atrocities; the people feel helpless in the face of the Government of India's inaction in dealing with the peccant officers, as the Imperial Government bade them do. The people see in Non-Co-operation a channel for their resentment, and eagerly seize it. The stirring up of race-hatred is, if possible, more immediately dangerous, than hatred of Government, and we have already seen one murder of an unarmed Englishman by four Musalmans armed with swords. The two who are arrested say that they committed the murder because of the Khilafat speeches. Such result was foreseen and, if Non-Co-operation is accepted as a principle, this one assassination will be the forerunner of many. It is no excuse to say that the murderers were bad characters; violence finds its tools among ignorant fanatics, not among high principled men. It is all very well for Mr. Gandhi to say that he feels no hatred against the Government he denounces, but only "absence of affection"; he may paralyse and yet be free from hatred, but those who follow him do not share his passivity, nor his self-control.

(iii) Non-Co-operation strikes at the foundation of Society which is based on Co-operation and can only exist through continued co-operation. It means a reversion to anarchy, a violent breaking of all the mutual ties which bind men together. It will inevitably lead to rioting and bloodshed, which can only have one result—repression and the putting off of all improvement in our civil conditions.

In practice, if I may be excused an Irish bull, it is impracticable. The moment a programme is proposed, the unanimous approval of "Non-Co-operation in principle" becomes a jangle of negatives against Non-Co-operation in practice. The political candidate refuses to boycott the Councils, the lawyer refuses to abandon his practice the parent declines to withdraw his children from school and college, an immense majority of title holders and men in honorary posts refuse to surrender them. After twenty-six days of proposed action in the Madras Presidency, 22 men had surrendered titles and honorary posts. The only point on which unanimity exists is in advice from those who have not to others who have, to make sacrifices. If such an infinitesimal result accrues, where the sacrifice is comparatively trifling, what will be the microscopic result when the second stage is reached and men are asked to surrender their livelihoods, and throw themselves and their families on the streets? Apart from Mr. Gandhi's programme, it is obvious that Non-Co-operation with Government implies an abandonment of all the conveniences which Government supplies. No one can buy a stamp, nor send a telegram nor travel by train, without contributing to the support of Government. No one can bring or defend a civil suit, nor register a document, without contributing to the support of Government. If courts are closed by Non-Co-operation, no redress can be had for assault, or robbery, or swindling, or forgery, or any other crime against person or property. Crops will perish for want of irrigation from Government-controlled canals. Famine will result from the stoppage of the transport of goods. Prices will rise yet higher from the same cause. Happily, the commonsense of the people will prevent them from rushing to destruction along the road opened to them. A very small number of the educated classes, judging by present appearances, will accept Mr. Gandhi's programme, though they will applaud him vociferously and cover him with inapposite and irrelevant praises for his saintliness, and profess unlimited reverence for him—strictly in principle.

People say, what will you propose in exchange? If I oppose a plan which leads to inevitable disaster and hopeless failure to attain its end, the fact that it is in itself ruinous and useless, is sufficient justification for the opposition. I see no immediate remedy for the Panjab atrocities, and, I say so honestly, I see no way for a real remedy short of Home Rule, and I would work the Reforms to the utmost so as to lessen the dangers of foreign rule. I would co-operate with the Government in all useful activities which would lesson poverty, improve industry, conserve the resources of the country for the country. I would utilise every scrap of power which the Reform Act gives, and by such success gain more, and so advance quickly towards Home Rule. I see no other way, and believing that the Non-Co-operation movement impedes our progress to Home Rule, may indefinitely delay its coming, and, in any case, by dividing the efforts of the people, weakens their power, I oppose Non-Co-operation as fervently and persistently as I work for Home Rule.
—*Looker-On.*

# AFTER THE CONGRESS

# THE BOYCOTT OF COUNCILS

By the Hon. Mr. R. P. Paranjpye

The Nationalists, especially in the Deccan, are saying that the resolution of the Congress incorporating the boycott of Councils as the first item in the programme of Non-Co-operation must have given great joy to the Liberals who are likely to find their way now clear to the seats in the Councils. Perhaps it is true that the boycott is likely to make the path of some Liberals easier; but it is simply cruel to say that they will welcome this result. The Liberals have consistently advocated the policy of making the reforms a success, and they know but too well that for this purpose the Councils have to be representative of the whole country and not merely of a party. The whole country is on a kind of trial for the next few years. The new Councils have to show that the responsibility thrown on them for the good administration of the country, such as it is, is properly borne, and that a distinct and visible amount of progress is made in the country during the next few years as a result of the reforms. For this purpose they know but too well that all the available ability in the country should be enlisted on the popular side, and they painfully realise that the quantum of this ability at present is not very great. Whatever some of the rabid organs of Extremism may say, nobody in his saner moments doubts that the Liberals have the good of the country at heart, though their methods may perhaps differ from those of their vivals. Their policy of working the reforms so as to get the utmost out of them requires the co-operation of all popular forces. It is only thus, they believe, that the permanent steady progress of the country can be assured, and not by any insane revolutionary methods.

For the last few months in the Deccan the Nationalists have been organising themselves as a party, and, making the

Amritsar resolution a shibboleth, have tried to discredit the Liberals, as they refuse to accept the opinion of the Congress on the reforms. At Sholapur they, in opposition to the Liberals, got the Provincial Conference to pass a resolution to this effect. The Liberals there contended, and they still feel that it for the present the best policy, that whatever one's views on the nature of the reforms may be, this policy is the soundest. The party machinery, however, continued to be manufactured. The Liberals in mere self-defence had to do the same. The contest for seats in the Councils bade fair to be very acrimonious and to be conducted on purely party lines. Many non-party men thought—and many saner party men on both sides agreed with them in their heart of hearts—that it would have been for the good of the country if a round table conference had been privately arranged to select the best candidates in the interests of the country and not in that of a party. The questions that are likely to crop up *in the immediate future* are such that both the Liberals and the Nationalists would have generally agreed upon them. This does not imply that there are, or will be, no differences. These differences are mainly of mental attitude, though, to a certain extent, they are due to personalities. As years roll on, the differences will crystallise the two parties. But crystallisation takes time. If the process is hastened, we shall have a large number of small crystals, while if time were allowed, larger crystals may be formed. This is what is happening now. In the Deccan several groups are manifesting themselves. The hand of everybody is against everybody else. If we had some actual experience of the new Councils to guide us, we should have seen where the vital differences, so far as Council work is concerned, lie and what will be the natural lines of cleavage and on what principles the public in the country will be divided into parties.

The Liberals were, and are, frankly out to work the reforms to the utmost. The attitude of the Nationalists who pronounce them unsatisfactory can be one out of the four following kinds. First, the attitude of taking the reforms as they are, sending the best men of the country irrespective of party to the Councils and then working them whole-heartedly so as to be able to show the greatest amount of actual successful work; secondly, contesting the elections on a purely party ticket, but after the elections are over, then working in co-operation with everybody who is on the side of the people; thirdly, contesting elections on the party ticket, refusing to co-operate with any one who is not of their own party and in fact following the methods roughly called obstructionist; fourthly, boycotting the Councils altogether. While the Liberals would have enthusiastically welcomed the first attitude, the second would not have left any bad after-effects except a rather less efficient personnel in the elected portion of the Councils. Before the Congress met, the saner Nationalists were in favour of this attitude; while the others were in favour of the third kind of attitude. The Congress has changed all this. It has given its orders to follow the fourth part. From the point of view of the successful working of the reformed Councils, it is obvious that this is less harmful than the purely obstructionist tactics. Even if the Nationalists had followed the second line, then Liberals who might come into the Councils would have been found on the whole working with them; the alliance—conspiracy as some Nationalists are pleased to call it—between the Liberals and the bureaucracy is a myth of the Extremist imagination. If the bureaucracy offers to co-operate, it will be suicidal to refuse the proferred hand; but the cause of the people, as against the party ought to be paramount both with the Liberals and the Nationalists; while therefore, as practical men, perhaps willing to accept compromise on current questions which involve no sacrifice of principle, the Liberals will be firm as as a rock on the main issues. We therefore again cordially exhort the Nationalists to reconsider their position and send their best men to the Councils, so that the popular side may have strength, not only of numbers, but capacity and ability and a fully representative character.

It appears, however, that in this Presidency, the Nationalists have decided to follow the Congress lead and boycott the Council elections. The Liberals will feel their strength reduced by this abstention. But may we appeal to the Nationalists to let the Councils work their own way and not to hamper their work? The Nationalists under the lead of Mr. Gandhi have chosen the path which they feel will lead them to the goal; is it too much to hope that they will allow others who believe in the other path, but who are not the less patriotic, to do their best in their own way without unnecessary hindrance?—*The Servant of India.*

# THE CALCUTTA CONGRESS

By C. P. Ramaswami Aiyar

The break with the past involved in the resolution adopted at the special session of the Congress is perhaps not recognised to the full even by those who helped to pass it. In the first place, some persons have been thinking and talking as if at Nagpur the Congress may again be set upon its old track of normal and constitutional agitation. Those who do so have ignored Art. XXVI of the Congress Constitution by which "no subject shall be pressed for discussion by the Subjects Committee or allowed to be discussed at the Congress by the President thereof to the introduction of which the Hindu or Muhammadan delegates as a body object by a majority of three-fourths of their number, and if, after discussion of any subject which has been admitted for discussion, it shall appear that the Hindu or Muhammadan delegates as a body are, by a majority of three-fourths of their number, opposed to the resolution which it is proposed to pass thereon, such resolution shall be dropped". To forget or to repeal this provision would be to strike at the roots of the Hindu-Muhammadan concord. If the provision is given effect to, it is evident that even if the Hindu delegates change their minds between now and December, the Muhammadans will not, and, indeed, after the attitude they have taken up, cannot alter their determination. It is thus demonstrable that for an indefinite period the non-co-operation doctrine must hold the field. What does this connote? It means that henceforth the Congress cannot address any representation or remonstrance to the Government; it cannot forward its opinion on any legislative or executive measure; it cannot protest to the authorities against any high-handed or arbitrary acts of officials; provincial and district Congress Committees cannot, as they have been doing in the past, handle local problems and try to remedy local troubles, and their sole function will be in their respective spheres to popularise and put into execution the ideas adumbrated by the Congress. Nor is this all. It is of course an elementary deduction from the resolution that the Congress can no longer play any part in the choice of representatives to the reformed legislative Councils. The various resolutions passed at provincial conferences as regards local organisations supporting the adherents of the Amritsar resolution *ipso facto* fall to the ground. The electoral arrangements made by the subordinate bodies affiliated to the Congress in certain Provinces have become obsolete, and committees of selection are futile and cannot function any further.

We recognise that, some time after the Congress had dissolved, individual members of the All-India Congress Committee at the close of a meeting of that body expressed the view that the resolution of the Congress is directory and not mandatory. But however advisory in character such a resolution might be, it will not justify the Congress or its subordinate organisations in any official capacity to act directly counter to the advice and suggestions of the present body, and indeed it is more than open to question how far it is within the competence of the All-India Congress Committee or the members thereof to proceed to expound and comment on the dicta of the Congress as they have attempted to do. Mr. Gandhi has become the law-giver for the Congress, but it is a well understood legal maxim that once the law is propounded the legislative authority cannot be invoked for the purpose of commenting on the law, especially where the commentary is opposed to the natural meaning of the enactment itself. Thus, therefore, the residual function of the Congress is the concentrated non-co-operation programme. Of course, Mr. Gandhi not only realises this circumstance but feels that at the present moment there is nothing else left to be done. But the warning may not be amiss in the case of those who, in some mysterious and confused fashion, desire to play the game of hide-and-seek with the doctrine. We hope we shall not be accused of cynicism when we point out that if the commentary of Pandit Madan Mohan Malaviya be accepted as an authoritative exposition of the Congress resolution it is open to every Congressman to accept new titles and offices and to make himself conspicuous at Darbars. All the items of advice are equally precatory or equally mandatory. If it is remembered that the struggle in the open Congress most fiercely raged around the introduction of the word "gradual" in certain parts of the resolution and its elimination in certain others, it is an absurd suggestion to say that the boycott of Councils can be ignored by "Congressmen," in the sense made familiar after the

Amritsar gathering. But if it is set at naught, two parts of the Congress resolution are deliberately flouted, namely, (1) that a beginning should be made by the classes who have hitherto moulded public opinion; and (2) that Non-Co-operation has been conceived as a measure of discipline and self-sacrifice.

The boycott of foreign goods now accepted as part of the resolution will bring about, if practised, such a revolution in our fiscal and commercial policy that it is difficult to estimate the likely consequences. The entire stoppage of the import of machinery in our nascent industrial condition is a contingency which it is not easy to contemplate without the gravest apprehensions. Compared with this, the boycott of Councils is a minor affair, but it is symptomatic of the psychology of the men assembled at Calcutta that two days in open Congress were devoted to a discussion of this topic, and from all accounts no one cared to trouble about the profound change in the economic and fiscal policy of the country.

We understand that certain legally-minded folk are oppressed with the idea that a portion of the resolution may offend against the newly passed Corrupt Practices Act. To inaugurate a revolution unique in character in the history of the world and yet to be afraid of a minatory provision in a measure designed to regulate elections is really to swallow the camel and strain at a gnat. The only explanation for the tactics displayed at the Calcutta Congress is that, save a few sincere adherents of Gandhi, the rest of them were playing at an elaborate make-believe. But in the pursuit of their game, it must not be forgotten that they have committed the Congress to a policy which renders it powerless for good in the present conditions, though potential for mischief uncontemplated by the originators of the new article of faith. For the first time in recent Indian political history has the issue become definite between two opposing parties—the one desirous of continuing more intensely and more sustainedly the older traditions of the Congress, and the other committed to an adventure, novel and full of sinister possibilities. Is it too much to ask that the situation must be clearly visualised and that all who are, by temperament and tradition, ranged on the one side or the other will try to follow the light that beats on their path with courage and without being oppressed by a false sense of party divisions? A re-adjustment of political vision and a reassortment of political parties is the need of the hour. To hesitate now would be to succumb weakly in the face of a dynamic propaganda whose results are only too easy to envisage.—*The Servant of India.*

---

## THE SPECIAL CONGRESS

By Annie Besant

The Special Congress has been held at Calcutta, and lasted from September 4th to September 8th, five days of strenuous work, partly in the Subjects Committee, partly in open sessions. It was a "Gandhi Congress". Both in the Subjects Committee and in the open Congress, he dominated the assemblies, and he finally carried his extraordinary resolution, and launched the Congress on a rapid current which will carry it to a National Niagara Falls.

It seems to me that all who are Congressmen will do well to pause and think at this critical moment, ere they enter on a course of decisive action, whither the road on which they enter will ultimately lead them—to National Self-Government or to National self-destruction. A study of the Congress at Calcutta will afford some useful and significant lessons, and it will be well to glance at them, at least, even if we cast them aside.

First, let us consider the constitution of the Congress. 5,873 delegates attended, of whom 2,100 were from Bengal. We cannot classify them under distinguishing labels, but we can judge of the temper of the majority by the Subjects Committee elected by the delegates. Very few, if any prominent, Moderates were elected. The President has the right to nominate five members; among these was one much respected Moderate from Madras, Dewan Bahadur L. A. Govindaraghava Iyer. The Hon. Mr. M. Ramachandra Rao was neither elected nor nominated, nor was he invited to speak, though I had handed in his name as a speaker against the Non-Co-operation resolutions. Quite young men made very violent speeches in the Congress, while experienced Moderates were ignored. Another testimony to the spirit of the delegates was the expulsion of

Mr. D. C. Ghose, who had voted against the withholding of advertisements from *The Statesman* in the Municipal Council, and of his father, Rai Bahadur Devender Chunder Ghose, one of the oldest members of the Congress. Members of the Reception Committee took part in abusing them, and when I was howled down they yelled at me "spy," and a "woman in the pay of the Government". Mr. Krishna Kumar Mitra wrote to the President asking him to place a resolution of censure before the Subjects Committee on those who had thus misbehaved, but nothing was heard of it. It must be remembered that the President-elect had specially invited some Moderate and National Home Rule leaders to come and had promised them a patient and respectful hearing. It was not in his power to obtain it. Mr. Jamnadas Dwarkadas, one of those who had received the invitation, was howled down. When I spoke against the Non-Co-operation resolution, I was greeted with a preliminary howl, but it quieted down, and I spoke very briefly in order to register my opposition, and did not attempt the reasoned speech which should be made at a Congress. It is clear that the Congress has become a purely party assembly, both in itself and in its organisations. The All-India Congress Committee and the Provincial Committees are of the Extreme Left, and as Lala Lajpat Rai said in his concluding speech, the refusal of a platform to the Moderates justified them in not attending the Congress, and the huge intolerant majority are reducing the National Congress to a purely party organisation. The Congress, in truth, is now nothing more. The old Congress is dead.

Next, let us consider the vote on the resolutions. The question was of vital National importance, and 5,873 men and women had gathered from all parts of India to decide this question. Should the Congress walk with accelerated pace on the path of Reform which had gained the Reform Act, inaugurating Responsible Government, or should it enter on the path of Revolution? Be it understood that there was no shrinking from the idea of Revolution; rather was it applauded: "a peaceful Revolution," "a bloodless Revolution," were phrases much applauded. "We declare war on the Government," a speaker cried. Under these circumstances one would have supposed that every delegate would have voted, compelled by a sense of responsibility, feeling his duty to his country. But only 2,778 delegates voted. Over 3,000 did not vote. Were they afraid to face abuse? They can hardly have been indifferent. Only 1,826 delegates voted for Mr. Gandhi's resolution, and by this microscopical fraction of the 245,000,000 of persons in the British *Raj* is the country flung into the fatal policy of Non-Co-operation. 884 voted for Mr. Bipin Chandra Pal's resolution. If of two impossibilities one can be more impossible than the other, his was the more impossible, for it would have completely stopped trade. 63 persons refused to vote for either resolution, but did their duty by attending, so as to register their rejection of the proposals which may plunge the country into riot and bloodshed, and, short of these, spread racial hatred, cause endless divisions, and block the path of progress and of freedom.

Mr. Gandhi's worst sin, now made a National disaster by the Congress, is in turning the attention of the country to this will-o'-the-wisp of Non-Co-operation from the fruitful devotion to strenuous political Reform. Just as the Congress is beginning to reap the fruit of its long labours, he snatches that fruit from its hand and turns the minds of the volatile people from patient work to wild excitement. The Home Rule propaganda gave the necessary impulse to earnest and strenuous work for the country. When that had awaked the National self-respect and pride, India's demand was met with recognition and the door of Home Rule was opened. We have in the Provinces responsible Ministers; the subjects most vital for the people are placed in their hands. Mr. Gandhi has led the younger men away from the path of work to the intoxication of "war against the Government," of hatred, and of inevitable failure and subsequent despair.

Is there not a better way? If the Editor will permit, I will suggest an answer next week.—*The Servant of India.*

---

## A BETTER WAY

By Annie Besant

I pointed out last week that the Congress had chosen to "enter on the path of Revolution," instead of walking "with accelerated pace on the path of Reform which had gained the

Reform Act, inaugurating Responsible Government." There is no doubt that during its thirty-five years of life, the Congress had trodden the latter path, and the awakened political consciousness of the country had only quickened the rate of progress; it had not changed the method. The Reform Act of 1919 is the legitimate child of the Minto-Morley Reforms, although it took a distinct step far in advance of its predecessor. But the Special Congress of 1920 has made a new departure; it has discarded political methods, declared its intention to paralyse the Government, and has created a "Council of Action," with Mr. Gandhi at its head. Under an impulse similar in kind to that which threatens to bring into conflict Labour and the Government in Great Britain, it has exchanged the Parliamentary method for that of Direct Action, alluring to the short-sighted with its promise of quick results. The sinister fact that Non-Co-operation can only succeed by violence is veiled from the myopic gaze. What cares the Government for the dropping of titles, the surrender of honorary posts, the abstinence from Councils, the withdrawal of children from schools, of lawyers from practice? All this will leave the withers of the Government unwrung. In fact the path will be the smoother for its feet. All the detail given is merely an expansion of the *first step* of Mr. Gandhi's fourfold programme, *the whole of which* was accepted in a previous paragraph on which no one laid any stress. It slipped through without notice. It is the three latter steps that, if successful, would paralyse the Government. It can look on smiling—though alert for the hidden danger—while the preliminary drill is going on.

The Better Way is to lay hold of the political power placed within our reach, to utilise it to the full with a clear objective, definitely stated and strenuously worked for—Full Responsible Government, Self-Government within the Commonwealth, Home Rule. The Premier said lately: "Britain is pledged to give India Home Rule." Mr. Montagu declared: "India will have Home Rule as soon as she is determined to have it." The determination must be proven by hard and efficient work within the Councils, producing and passing well-considered measures for the lessening of poverty by the improvement of agriculture and increase of irrigation, the stimulation of industrial undertakings, and also spread of cottage industries, aided by co-operative societies, the uplift of the people by education, the lessening of disease by sanitation and instruction in hygiene. These and similar measures should be explained to the masses, pointed to as the results of power coming into Indian hands, so that they may feel the reaction on their own lives of even partial Home Rule. Local Self-Government must be boldly established, with elected Village, Taluq, and District Councils, and the Village Panchayat must control village affairs, with its Committees of Education, Water-Supply, Justice, Revenue, etc., as needed according to the size of the village, as in former days. The Taluq Council will control roads outside villages, Secondary Schools, larger irrigation, will have its model Farm and Dairy, and act as a distributing centre for stud animals, seeds, manures, disposal of surplus products, etc. The District Council will have its College, its Technical Institute, its Agricultural Institute with experts, making experiments, testing soils and suitable manures, suitable crops, supplying seeds, rendering available to every village through the Taluq Board the best scientific knowledge of the day. The whole rural life of the people may thus be transformed, and they will become politically educated by the use of power in their villages, by the inevitable discussion and growing sense of responsibility. Village self-government is our new basis, it being remembered that the village officers must be elected, not appointed. Some very successful experiments have been made in Bengal and Lord Ronaldshay lately pointed with great satisfaction to the fact that the villagers were very ready to tax themselves for village improvements when they controlled the work and the expenditure; they found that they could do the work more cheaply than the Public Works Department.

The Provincial Councils will pass the legislation necessary for Local Self-Government: they will deal with hours of Labour, Arbitration Courts, Provincial Taxation and Expenditure, Town Planning, Housing Schemes, and all matters of larger organisation concerning the Province as a whole. Surely the great vistas opening before us may well call out the best brains and hearts to work for India, and to build up every story of the great edifice of Home Rule, carrying the people with them by knowledge worked out in practice, uplifting and transforming their lives. We shall not need to ask for Home Rule; we shall create it, rendering it inevitable. We shall mould the Government and make it ours, carrying out Mr. Gokhale's famous maxim: "Co-operation where possible, opposition where necessary," but we shall co-operate and resist with power, not in weakness as of yore.

Is not this a Better Way than Mr. Gandhi's dreary, quarrelsome way of Non-Co-operation, raising racial hatred, making cleavage after cleavage, our enemies ever those who are of our own household. Surely we can thus better serve the motherland, better help our brethren, crown our India with Home Rule, winning it by work which in itself is joyous and will gladden the homes of the land. Co-operation is our watchword; Co-operation with each other, Co-operation with the Government, Co-operation in every good and great and noble work. We will not stand aside in dull and sullen, resentful and idle Non-Co-operation, but will take hands and work, knowing that the future is our own.—*The Servant of India.*

---

## NON-CO-OPERATION

By Ambika Charan Majumdar

Although lying on my sick bed I am dragging on a dead-alive existence, useless alike to myself and to the public, I have been following with grave anxiety the trend of events in the country during the past twelve months and more. While the "pros" and "cons" of the Montagu-Chelmsford reforms were being hotly discussed in the country, the harrowing disturbances in the Panjab and the dismemberment of the Turkish Empire burst like bomb shells to unsettle the public mind and aggravate the situation. But with the Special Session of the Congress just held in Calcutta that situation has reached its climax, and every thoughtful mind in the country is now swayed by alternate feelings of hope and despair not only for the success of the coming reforms, but also for the future of the country. In a democratic organisation which has so far been conducted on constitutional lines, a bold and venturesome leader has raised the standard of revolt, which for the time being has captured the imagination of a section of immature youthful minds, and struck at the very foundation of constitutional political agitation in the country. Mr. M. K. Gandhi has given his fiat for Non-Co-operation, apparently regardless of its inevitable consequences, which, if seriously accepted by the country, threatens either to paralyse the great National organisation which has so far moulded the destiny of the country, or what is worse, tear it off from its old moorings and drift it on in dangerous waters to ultimately shatter it on invisible rocks ahead. It may be no offence to say that in the making of the Congress Mr. Gandhi and most of his enthusiastic followers had clearly no hand, and for its achievements they are naturally left uninspired with any sentiment of either respect or admiration, although it was conceived, nurtured and developed by a class of Mahatmas many of whom, though they have been gathered to their fathers, still inspire the public mind and serve as a beacon light for public guidance. If Mr. Gandhi really meant to preach a new cult and demonstrate the utter futility of the Congress methods, he would have been well advised to start an independent organisation better suited to his higher ideals, rather than forcibly wreck one for which he was not at all responsible, and to whose constitution he owed little or no allegiance. That would have been more intelligible and consistent with his principle and practice. Though Mr. Gandhi has carried the day by his singular personality, largely taking advantage of the exasperated and unsettled condition of the public mind, particularly among impressionable and immature young men, it is evident from what has since transpired that he has not won more than a Pyrrhic victory, over which a man like him cannot afford to be either proud or exultant; for it is abundantly clear that in spite of the Congress resolution that he has carried, there is an overwhelming volume of thinking and responsible public opinion in the country which is emphatically opposed to his idealistic propaganda. Not to speak of the tried old veterans in the Moderate party, even among the more sober and level headed stalwarts of his own camp there has arisen a sharp cleavage which it is not possible for him either to flout or to ignore. If Mr. Gandhi persists in his movement, it is not difficult to foresee that the inevitable result of such a movement will be to make the Extremists of to-day the Moderates of to-morrow. Let him ponder over the situation, and, the sincere and honest man that he is, let him place his hand upon his heart and say to himself, if not to the public, whether

9

his mandate is being ungrudgingly and whole-heartedly accepted by the more important and responsible section of the Extremists in the country, and if his propaganda can be carried on to a successful issue without their hearty co-operation, or with the mere help of a handful of irresponsible young men, who are scarcely able to realise the true significance of that propaganda and the gravity of the present situation. Is the country to understand that his policy of Non-Co-operation extends also to these important men and that he is prepared to do even without them? Everybody who is any body in the country resents the Panjab outrages and the whole country, irrespective of party and creed, has been unanimous in its verdict of condemnation of the Amritsar massacre. But the question is: Is Non-Co-operation, such as has been enunciated by Mr. Gandhi, the proper remedy for the removal of these and other wrongs from which the country has been patiently suffering so long? Or is it not the fact that it is only by active participation in the administration and gradual assumption of power and control over all the departments of the State, that we can effectively redress such wrongs, or prevent their repetition in future? I would like to put the issue more plainly. Home Rule, Self-Government, or "Swaraj," by whatever name one may choose to call it, our sole aim is to attain autonomous independence. Now history tells us throughout the world that independence, whether within or without, an Empire can only be achieved in one of the following three ways, *viz*: (1) by rebellion, (2) by revolution, and (3) by the process of evolution. Non-Co-operation cannot be an End, but it can only be used as "a means to an End". Now the End being admittedly "independence" can it be gained by Non-Co-operation, unless the aim of such Non-Co-operation be either rebellion or revolution? I would pause for a reply. If Mr. Gandhi and his followers intend to resort either to the 1st or the 2nd method, let them plainly say so, and the country will understand them clearly and decide whether or not to accept this propaganda. He and his new cult would then be more intelligible. It is no use, perhaps it is more harmful than useless, to try to darken the real issue under cover of sensational rhetoric, and attempt to capture imaginative minds with empty platitudes, which can serve only to inflame the passions and misguide the judgment of the unwary public. If neither of these two alternatives is open to us, then it is evident that

Non-Co-operation is not only meaningless, but positively harmful to the achievement of our admitted aim of independence. If we have to rely on constitutional efforts to evolve our destiny, as we have done so far, then, barring rebellion or revolution, there remains evolution as our only weapon to attain our desired object, however slow and tedious the process may be. We have no doubt to a large extent exhausted our patience without any adequate return for our labours, but if evolution is still to be our method, we can only take such measures as would accelerate the pace of that evolution, and not unconsciously and unwarily drift to other methods which are not open to us, and which if aimed at can only end in disaster and ruin. By "Co-operation" it is not meant that we should enter into an *entente cordiale*, and practise slavish hob-a-nobbing with the bureaucrat, but active participation in every department of the State in a spirit of perfect independence, and with loyalty to the country and respect for the constitution, so that by gradually assuming effective control over the State we may be able to exclude and eliminate that bureaucracy which is regarded as the bane of the present administration and against which we all so loudly complain. In short Co-operation is intended to work from within, while Non-Co-operation is bound to work from without. It is in the nature of evolution that every thing must be done from within, while it is the essence of effective Non-Co-operation that it must work from without. Work we must, whether from within or from without, if our object be to work out our salvation. We have so long persistently, though vainly knocked at the gate, and now when the gate has been nearly opened, is it wise to turn away sulkily in a fit of temper and say: No, we shall not enter the citadel but storm it with long-range guns from a distance?

It is alleged that the movement will be one of "non-violent peaceful Non-Co-operation". I frankly confess that I am unable to reconcile this incongruous and inconsistent paradox. Such a movement is unpractical and impracticable. According to Mr. Gandhi's interpretation Non-Co-operation in its proper analysis resolves only into a political hunger-strike, and political hunger-strike is the most cowardly form of committing political suicide. Perfectly passive Non-Co-operation can only achieve the political "Nirvana" of a people, but not its political salvation. We cannot forget that the same thing was said with regard to Mr. Gandhi's Hartal and Satyagraha movements, but how disastrously they failed and ended in a massacre of the innocents is still fresh in our memory. Mr. Gandhi's bitter experiences of the past should have made him wiser for the future. He may unconsciously deceive himself, but I am sure he is not the man consciously to deceive others. He is certainly not the man who is capable of saying in light heart: "Mischief, thou art afoot, take what course thou wilt". The last special session of the Congress was undoubtedly a packed assembly in which neither the constitution of that body nor its established methods and procedure were very much observed, and it is deeply to be regretted that some of our best men should have found it obligatory on their part to abide by its mandate, even though such mandate went wholly and decisively against their settled conviction. Loyalty to the Congress may be an admirable virtue, but if any particular session of the Congress goes out of its way and passes a decision, not only in contravention of its settled policy and creed, but also in absolute disregard of the best interests of the country, then should every man who steps inside such an assembly be bound hand and foot even by its perverse decision? Supposing at the next annual session of the Congress at Nagpur Mr. Gandhi were to go a step further, and as a corrollary to his original proposition were to lay down that as a palliative for the privation which is likely to result from his passive Non-Co-operation movement, every Congressman should practise the austere principle of living on one meal a day or one meal in two days. I ask in all seriousness if men like Mr. B. Chakravarti or Mr. C. R. Das would feel themselves bound by such an absurd resolution? Many of us had fondly hoped that however defective and disappointing the initial stage of the reforms might be, the best men in the country, whether Moderates or Extremists would rally round them and by their united efforts acting and reacting on the defective constitution serve to strength on it and accelerate the pace of progress towards the destined goal. Unfortunately however the attitude of some of our best men has been more "unsatisfactory and disappointing" than the reforms themselves. No one doubts Mr. Gandhi's intense patriotism; but patriotism, however intense or genuine, unless guided by the wand of reason and controlled by political sagacity, is bound to degenerate into morbid sentimentality which can serve only to conjure up visions and produce hallucination. The idea of making the administration impossible by mere Non-Co-operation seems to be grotesque under the existing condition of things. It may be possible to do so in a free country, and it may be possible even here, after we have passed a certain stage; but to attempt passive Non-Co-operation in this country at the present moment, when we have neither the means to enforce our demands ncr to stand on our own legs, can end only in disastrous consequences. The administration has gone on for more than 30 years without the Co-operation of Congressmen, and it is idle to expect that the Government will come down on its knees upon our adopting a perfectly passive attitude such as peaceful Non-Co-operation can only mean. To my young countrymen who have apparently grown impatient of old leadership, as being unprogressive and autocratic, I would only say: Let them beware that in their admiration for the new, they do not behave like the Roman citizens, who for extolling Brutus and denouncing Cæsar ended by crying out: "Let him be Cæsar."—*The Bengalee.*

---

## NON-CO-OPERATION

By G. A. Natesan

In adopting the Resolution on Non-Co-operation on the terms adumbrated by Mr. Gandhi, the Indian National Congress has committed the country to a course of conduct which is sooner or later bound to produce calamitous consequences. It is sad to contemplate that despite the opposition of the entire body of the Moderate party, and of several of the leaders of the Congress like Pandit Madan Mohan Malaviya, Mrs. Besant and others, a wrong lead has been given to the country. For this deplorable decision the Nationalists who till recently shouted loud for a policy of Non-Co-operation are themselves to blame. Mr. Gandhi has from the beginning been led to believe that the entire body of Nationalists were with him in support of his policy. It is not surprising that at the last moment some of the Nationalist leaders began to open their eyes and realised the danger of his programme. Mr. Gandhi—to whom there could be no compromise between right and wrong, and to whom no considerations of expediency could appeal in matters of conscience—refused to yield to the entreaties of his friends and persisted in carrying out his programme. It is but natural that the large body of Congressmen —the thousands drawn from all classes and creeds who had assembled in Calcutta, before whom the new and fascinating weapon had been brandished so often—should prefer the lead of Mr. Gandhi, "a personality based on a life of service, an exalted patriotism and a moving idealism," and refuse to be guided by leaders who have been waiting to be led by their followers, and have by their vacillating and dubious conduct brought ridicule if not contempt on themselves.

What more demoralising than that Nationalist leaders who bravely fought against the boycott of Councils in open Congress, urging amongst other sound reasons the strongest of all, that it would be an act of political suicide, should the very next day proclaim their withdrawal from elections and begin once again to talk and write glibly of Non-Co-operation? And this *volte-face*, we are told, is in the name of the solidarity of the Congress; and surely one would expect them to realise in the name of common sense that the country was undoubtedly greater than the Congress itself.

We admit that the grave wrongs inflicted on the people of the Panjab are wrongs inflicted on the people of India. We admit that the seventy millions of Musalmans and with them their Hindu brethren have every reason to feel indignant that the spoken word of the British Premier should have been thrown away to the winds. We own with others that life has been rendered galling. Something effective should be done to make the Government of India understand that by its conduct, particularly in the Panjab episode, it has brought its administration into contempt, and that it has consciously or unconsciously done everything in its power to accelerate the speed with which the trust of the people in the good faith of the rulers is being shaken.

If we thought that in the best interests of the country the Non-Co-operation programme of Mr. Gandhi, sanctified by the authority of the Congress, would serve the purpose of righting the wrongs of the Panjab, obtain a revision of the Turkish treaty and help the attainment of full responsible Government, we should be happy to support it. But we feel strongly that the movement will defeat the very object it has in view; and that though started with the honest intention of being worked in a non-violent spirit it is likely to lead to violence. Depriving the growing youth of the country of the benefits of education, deserting the Courts where innocent men are often on their trial, and boycotting of Councils by the best and most talented of Indians, and that in a field where there is undoubtedly great scope for patriotism and self-sacrifice; measures like these are in our humble judgment calculated to put off the day when responsible government is likely to be won. It is a perilous policy to which the Congress has committed the country: and Congress or no Congress, it is the duty of all who disapprove of this movement to protest and work against it.

At the same time we feel it our duty to point out that the authorities will be greatly mistaken if they believe that Non-Co-operation will perish of its inanity. Every fresh blunder of the bureaucracy will add to its strength, and bureaucracy has a fatal facility for blundering. It may not be immediately possible for the authorities to obtain a satisfactory settlement of the Khilafat problem. But it is in their power to prove their good faith to the Indian public by dealing out condign punishment to the officials in the Panjab, who have brought dishonour to their name. We must finally own that the tension of the situation will be greatly relieved by replacing the present head of the Government in India, whose ineptitude has brought us to this unfortunate pass.—*The Indian Review.*

---

## NON-CO-OPERATION AND OUR DUTY

### AN APPEAL TO OUR COUNTRYMEN

By Sir A. Chaudhuri, Satyananda Bose, J. N. Roy, J. Chaudhuri, and B. C. Chatterji

Bengal has arrived at a momentous crisis of its history. The hour is come for its choosing between the maintenance of its intellectual and political integrity and the surrender of its reason and leadership to a political chimera. All Bengal is united in its determination to achieve full and complete Swaraj as soon as possible; the speeches at the last session of the Special Congress leave little doubt that all the leaders of the political thought of the Province are further united in regarding the reformed legislative Councils as valid and effective instruments for quickening the pace of the Nation towards the great goal. In the midst of this unity of purpose and method the monster of a futile but tragic dissension has suddenly raised its head. Some of Bengal's leading representatives have withdrawn their candidature for the Council in obedience to the resolution of the majority at the Special Congress, although they had opposed the passing thereof with all the strength and earnestness they could command. We apprehend that their withdrawal from the elections is founded upon a misunderstanding of the nature and authority of Congress resolutions. Mr. Gandhi, we venture to think, showed a clearer appreciation of the position by stating at the beginning of his memorable speech that in the event of the majority deciding against him, he would regard himself entirely free to go on with his programme against their resolution. The essence of the Congress proceedings has been their elasticity, the majority never wishing or attempting to enforce their decision on the minority on the analogy of a legislative enactment. As Mr. Gandhi observed, the aim of a dissenting minority in a particular session of the Congress should be to convert itself into a majority at the forthcoming one; but this very object would be, more often than not, defeated, if the minority were in the meanwhile to carry out the will of the majority in the spirit of submission to a law. The question of boycotting the Councils would serve as an useful illustration. A series of majority decisions at the forthcoming session of the Congress in favour of its members entering the Councils would serve no practical purpose; whereas the harm entailed in the procedure we are deprecating would be much intensified if at the session of the Congress immediately preceding the next elections, Mr. Gandhi were to succeed by one of his supreme efforts in registering another majority vote against entry into the Councils. We yield to none in our loyalty to the Congress. We shall always be in it and of it; it shall ever be to us the inspiration and the symbol of our national determination to be free; the sacred meeting ground of India's sons and daughters as brothers and sisters; the holy tabernacle wherein we shall yearly renew our oath of allegiance to the Mother, our vow of self-dedication to her service for the length of our life. But we would earnestly plead with our countrymen not to lead the great institution along the path of futility by treating it as though it were a legislative body, which it is not.

We would also appeal to our countrymen not to dismiss the new Government of India Act in a spirit of light-heartedness, but rather would we ask them to appraise this enactment at its real worth by examining into the circumstances of its causation. Surely Great Britain did not declare responsible government to be the goal of British Indian policy on the 20th August, 1917, in a fit of absent-mindedness. The study of her history warrants no such supposition. The hour of that declaration was overdue, and she made it because she realised in a luminous moment of chastened experience that she needs must, or break up her Empire of which India was a vital and organic part. Behind that declaration and the legislation that has followed it, lies the whole history of modern India: all the aspiration and the activity of the founders and followers of the Indian National Congress, all the dreaming and daring, the faith and the hope and the determination, the burning intolerance of unfreedom, the passionate self-sacrifice, summed up in the single phrase "Young India"; the memory of men who have been through durance and exile with a smile, of those who have passed to their rest from the gallows with "Bande Mataram" on their unquivering lips; the splendid heroism of India's Kshattriyas who have died on the fields of England's Empire for the redemption of their country's shame. All this nobility of endeavour has gone to the making of the new character, which we should succeed in seeing in its correct perspective, if only we could discipline ourselves to look not merely into our immediate present, but also into our immediate past. Doing so, we should light upon the outstanding message of Aurobindo Ghose, that India must accept partial SWARĀJ as a means and step towards complete SWARĀJ. This gifted son of Bengal combined in himself the vision of the seer with the sanity of the statesman, and was able ten years ago to anticipate and visualise to himself the broad outlines of the events that have since happened, and thus leave corresponding words of guidance for his countrymen. We quote the following from his famous

"Political Will and Testament," published in the *Karmo Yogin*, on the eve of his departure for Pondichery. "It is generally supposed that the Nationalist party is committed to the persistent and uncompromising refusal of co-operation until they get the full concession of Swarāj. Nationalist publicists have not cared to combat this error explicitly because they were more anxious to get their ideal accepted and the spirit of passive resistance and complete self-help popularised, than to discuss a question which was not then a part of practical politics. But it is obvious that a party advancing such a proposition would be a party of doctrinaries and idealists, not of practical thinkers and workers. The Nationalist principle is the principle of 'no control, no co-operation'. Since all control has been refused and so long as all control is refused, the Nationalist party preaches the refusal of co-operation as complete as we can make it. But it is evident that if, for instance, the power of imposing protective duties were given to a popular and elective body, no serious political party would prefer persistence in commercial boycott to the use of the powers conceded. Or if education were similarly made free of official control and entrusted to a popular body, as Lord Reay once thought of entrusting it, no sensible politician would ask the nation to boycott that education. Or if the courts were manned by Indian judges and made responsible not to the Executive but to a Minister representing the people, arbitration would immediately take its place as a supplementary aid to the regular courts. So also the refusal to co-operate in an administration which excludes the people from an effective voice does not involve a refusal to co-operate in an administration of which the people are an effective part. The refusal of autocratic gifts does not involve a refusal to take up popular rights inalienably secured to the people. It is, on the contrary, with the object of compelling the concession of the various elements of Swarāj by peaceful moral pressure and in the absence of such concessions developing our own institutions to the gradual extrusion and final supplanting of bureaucratic institutions, that the policy of self-help and passive resistance was started. The acceptance of popular rights does not imply the abandonment of the ideal of complete autonomy, or of the use of passive resistance in case of any future arbitrary interference with the rights of the people. It implies only the use of partial Swarāj as a step and means towards complete Swarāj."

We subscribe to every word of this remarkable pronouncement. The statesman in him made him aware that Indian freedom like the Empire of Rome could not be built in a day, and would come to his country by way of partial Swarāj, which he admonished his countrymen not to forgo unless they were content for ever with the rule of being mere doctrinaires and idealists. None has a greater right to speak on behalf of the Motherland than he, and we are loth to believe that his countrymen will not seriously take to heart and act upon those pregnant words he has left behind him, applying literally, as they do, to the facts of the present situation. The very prescience of which they were born should inspire us to follow them. Had Parliament transferred the control to the popular representatives over no more than the department of education, Aurobindo Ghose would have his countrymen cease to non-co-operate to the extent of such control; his call to Co-operation becomes therefore of the greater urgency and authority in view of the transference of control to the people's nominees over so many more branches of Government. It is not without reason that men like Pulin Behary Das and others of like faith, who have suffered so much for the sake of the love they have borne the Motherland, have expressed themselves explicitly against the doctrine and practice of Non-Co-operation In the highest interests of the Motherland, in the light of all the happenings since Swadeshi, and in the words of one of India's noblest sons, we would conclude with the earnest appeal to our contrymen to take up the task of partial Swarāj in that spirit of concentration and consecration, which alone can lead it into the fruition of complete Swarāj the fixed and unalterable goal of our common aspiration and common endeavour.—*The Bengalee.*

---

## A LETTER ON NON-CO-OPERATION

By THE HON. MR. BHURGRI

DEAR Mr. Haji Abdullah—I am in receipt of your letter of the 23rd instant.

I am surprised and sorry to find that so much misapprehension should exist respecting the position of honest dissenters from the policy of Non-Co-operation. This would not be if there were a clearer understanding of the real issues involved.

I take it that the case for Non-Co-operation is that the settlement of the Khilafat question involved in the Turkish peace treaty is a grievance of the Musalmans; that the Khilafat being a sacred institution, it is the religious duty of all true Musalmans to endeavour to obtain a redress of that grievance; that the grievance can only be redressed by obtaining Self-Government for India, to put the scheme at its lowest; and that the only means to this end is Non-Co-operation.

Now, I am prepared to grant that the Khilafat is a religious question, and that it is the duty of every loyal Musalman to support it. I also agree that the best way to advance that cause is to obtain Self-Government for India. But the question still remains as to the ways and means of achieving Self-Government. I think there can be no doubt that this is purely a secular and political question. In this view, the religious element is, therefore, altogether irrelevant to the only issue involved. The end is clear and undisputed, and that is Self-Government. The only question is the choice of the means to that end. This, I would again repeat, is entirely non-religious in character. On this subject every individual is entitled to his own opinion, including the doctors of the faith, whose opinions are, however, entitled to no greater weight than the opinions of other private citizens. It is, therefore, to my mind, perfectly unreasonable, unfair and futile to introduce religious considerations in a matter which is purely secular. The goal of both non-co-operators and their opponents is identical. It is Self-Government for India. It is only the routes chosen by the two parties that are divergent.

Now the three main ways to this goal are open violence, Non-Co-operation and constitutional agitation. Open violence has no partisans, not even among those doctors of the faith who are prepared to hold that a "jehad" is a justifiable weapon with which to avenge or redress any injury to the cause of religion. It is presumably discredited because it is regarded as impracticable. Then comes Non-Co-operation, or withdrawal of association with the administration in every direction for the purpose of crippling and paralysing it. Now let us examine the merits and prospects of this policy a little more closely than is wont to be done.

The first steps of the Non-Co-operation policy are the boycott of Councils, the boycott of schools, and the boycott of foreign goods. First as to the boycott of the Councils. This scheme will neither work nor pay. To count on such a course is to reckon without your host. For one man that avoids election, there will be several to seek it. It is idle to expect that the Councils will remain empty. They will be filled somehow of a certainty. To know this needs but a small knowledge of human nature. However, even if this policy did work to a certain extent, it would assuredly not pay. It would keep away precisely the most fitted and most useful, and put in their places not only the least deserving and least serviceable, but the most mischievous and most dangerous. Would this be a service or a disservice to the country? Would this not frustrate instead of furthering, the one great common National purpose of Self-Government? Would not the very "success" of the Council boycott be the greatest failure? The bureaucracy would only stand to gain by the support of those who would be only too ready to play into their hands. I quite agree that the effect of such a scheme would be to cripple and paralyse. But the party so affected would be, not the Government but the people themselves.

Next as to the boycotting of schools. I do not think any measure could be more gratuitous and mischievous than this. It is absolutely uncalled for—inasmuch as the people are asked to deprive themselves of the benefit of what they pay for, as it is the tax-payers' money that eventually supports the schools. The present system of education may be defective, and greatly defective. But to say that it is wholly useless is certainly to say far too much. It must never be forgotten that the very development in men and affairs that is our pride and our hope to-day is a product of it. Education is the one great need of the country. It is the special need of the Muslim community, particularly in Sindh. The condition of the Muhammadans in this Province is an instructive object-lesson on the grave drawbacks attending an attitude of indifference or hostility to education. On every side efforts are being made to promote this great cause as much as possible. Free and compulsory education has been the object for which every Indian patriot has been striving. The Reforms have given the administration of education to the people's representatives as a transferred subject, and have opened up splendid opportunities for the greatest progress. And now the people are asked in the same breath to sever their connection with the schools. No care is taken that there is or will be immediate and adequate provision for the education of the children so withdrawn. There are neither in *esse* nor in proximate *posse* other schools, sufficient in number and satisfactory in quality, to meet the requirements. A long time must elapse before properly equipped schools are fully available without the aid of Government.

The boycott of foreign goods is also a most impracticable and prejudicial scheme. It will scarcely work at all, and, if it does, it will do more harm to indigenous industry than to foreign. Besides, this is one of those matters which it is easier to preach than to practise. Very little heart-searching will suffice to show how hollow are such professions when brought to the test of sacrifice. I imagine the numbers of those who are ready to close down their business, which means profit, at the call of principle, which means loss, are very few indeed. I would only ask every advocate of Non-Co-operation to apply this test to himself to prove the sincerity and strength of his convictions. I shall be very much mistaken if the vast majority are not found wanting when tried in this balance. To come nearer home, I shall be greatly surprised to hear that any merchant in Sindh has closed his business in foreign goods.

On the merits and prospects of any further steps of the Non-Co-operation policy, namely, withdrawal from the Army police and other services, and the non-payment of taxes, it is unnecessary to dwell at any length. They are so obviously impracticable and prejudicial in character as to be scarcely in need of refutation.

The renunciation of titles and honorary offices is a matter of comparatively trivial importance, the success or failure of which is of no consequence whatever. However, the feebleness of the response in this small matter is an instructive commentary on the prospects of the bigger items of the programme.

I have been at some pains to show that the only question before the people is that course which is mostly likely to promote the general cause of the country. My next position is that this is a question which every individual must ask and decide for himself with all the sincerity and courage that are in him. I beg to dissent from the view that the mere opinion of a majority should override the honest and deliberate opinion of a considerable and enlightened minority in all classes, under all circumstances and irrespective of all considerations.

There are matters and occasions on which every individual must think out for himself. This is not only his clear right, but his plain duty. I do not subscribe to the doctrine that a man's association with a body operates as a merger of his whole individuality and the disposal of his mind and soul and conscience. This is a doctrine that was boldly repudiated by the greatest of all statesmen, Edmund Burke, in his memorable address to his electors, who sought to place their interests above the dictates of his conscience and the welfare of the country. I, too, while a member, and a loyal and zealous member, of the Congress, make bold to reserve to myself my own liberty of conscience and to place its dictates above the decision of that body. I am not the only one who so thinks and feels. I am happy to think that, though in a minority, I am in the best of company, composed of the intellect and experience of the country. I feel fortified by the opinion of one of India's greatest sons, whose reputation for wisdom, honesty, patriotism and independence is above reproach, Pandit Mohan Malaviya, who, though a distinguished and veteran member of the Congress dissents from this policy of Non-Co-operation, and has given open expression to his views on the subject in his recent speech at Calcutta. In this connection, it is idle to cite instances of men who have waived their opposition to Non-Co-operation in submission to the decision of the Congress. I, with many others, feel that they have failed in their duty in so doing. At any rate, their action is the result of their own judgment, and cannot be held up as an example to others who think and feel differently.

To any considerations personal to myself, I am perfectly indifferent. My position in the country has been sufficiently established. I was the first Musalman to enter the Congress, amidst the howls and curses of my co-religionists. For many years I was among the small number of Musalmans who took active part in National politics. I was the first Musalman member of the Home Rule League in Sindh when that association was despised and decried. I can, therefore, justly claim to be one of the pioneers of my community in the domain of politics. I have always held to my principles with honesty, strength and courage, in spite of criticism, slander, abuse, and even persecution. And I am happy to find that time and progress have been my vindication. I have fought a long and strenuous battle with the bureaucracy on many an issue. I am still as ardent a Congressman and Home-Ruler as ever before. If I disagree with a certain decision of the Congress, it is not because I am disloyal, but because I honestly feel that that decision is prejudicial to the very interests that the Congress espouses and the very purpose the Congress has in view. Those interests are the interests of the Indian people and that purpose is Self-Government. I feel that the country's cause will best be served by the best men and the largest number getting into the Councils, there to work out the policy of Self-Government for India. I sincerely believe there is great scope for good work in the new Councils. To take only one instance. The Reforms have made over the management of education to the people. This may be made the means of achieving the greatest result in the way of compulsory education. This one measure, if it comes to pass through the co-operation of the people and their representatives, will be worth infinitely more than all the supposed good that Non-Co-operation promises to achieve. It is only for this reason that I am seeking election to the Council of State. My one intention and desire are to contribute my humble quota to the great work before the people. It is not from any petty purpose of vanity or prestige that I am acting. My one and only motive is service to the country. I am not enamoured of the Councils. I have shown that they are not the be-all and end-all of my existence. I was among the first to resign my seat on the Provincial Council. In so acting, I obeyed the call of my conscience, and not the will of party. I then thought that as the peace terms were under discussion, strong pressure from the Musalmans might result in a better settlement. But now that the Peace Treaty has been signed by Turkey, there is no hope for any revision in the near future, whether the Councils be boycotted or not. It is therefore that I have decided to stand.

The opposition that is threatened, I am quite prepared for and indifferent to. I am standing up for a principle, and am not merely out for result. Success or failure does not concern me. I think there is greater merit and glory in losing in an honest fight in a good cause, than in flying from the field through weak fear on timid compliance. I shall at least have the sanction of my own conscience and the approval of all honest men. I know it would be much the easier and pleasanter course for me to withdraw from the field. I should be glorified as a hero. But this cheap heroism makes no appeal to me. It is no part of my policy to be merely playing to the tune of any party, whether it be the bureaucracy or the people. Principle is my only guide, and to vindicate it I am ever ready to fight any party opposed to it, whether it be the bureaucracy or the people and even though the fight be a losing fight. To this end I have been putting my position clearly and truthfully before my electors. False pretences and professions are no part of my game. The allegation that my agents are posing me as representative of the Khilafat is absolutely false and unfounded. Any such attempts would be unreasonable and foolish, as the fraud would be speedily exposed by the Khilafat party. No; my methods are, and will always be, perfectly legitimate and straight. With the methods of my opponents I am not concerned. I only feel that it would be in their own interests to abstain from a compaign of intimidation, coercion and abuse. Such methods are only apt to recoil on those that pursue them. They cannot affect persons who fight fair and are prepared to lose. I disagree openly, but I am neither afraid nor shamed. In my view, there is such a thing as honest disagreement and candid dissenters are always entitled to respect. It is not the substance, but the character, of the opinion that really matters. In the present case, even the substance of the opinion against Non-Co-operation is worthy of respect. Pressure in any form never really advanced any cause, and the cause of Non-Co-operation is no exception to the rule.—*The New Times.*

---

## NON-CO-OPERATION AND MR. GANDHI

By N. M. SAMARTH

It is to be hoped that British statesmen and British publicists, of whatever political persuasion, will appreciate, in its true perspective, the deplorable situation which has arisen in India, and which has resulted in the adoption of Mr. Gandhi's "Non-Co-operation" programme by a majority of the delegates who voted on it at the special session of the Indian National Congress recently held at Calcutta. Some are apt to exaggerate the gravity of the situation, in order to justify a policy of severe repression—a policy which would never allay but would assuredly aggravate the situation. Others may be inclined to belittle its significance, so that no serious notice may be taken of the underlying causes which have gradually brought it about. While the latter would look upon the present state of things in India as a mere passing phase of Indian agitation, which is bound to fizzle out in course of time, the former would account for it solely as the result of the pernicious activity of Indian Extremists, who deserve to be repressed and suppressed with a high hand. Either will be a mistaken view.

Mr. Gandhi is not an Extremist in the sense in which that term is generally applied and understood in Indian politics. Indian Extremists, rightly viewed, are Indian patriots in an angry mood. That mood necessarily postulates absence of coolheadedness. Mr. Gandhi is nothing if not cool-headed. He is an idealist, pure and simple—an idealist with an unshakable faith in adamantine "soul-force," as the only force opposed to physical force which can compel the most powerful Government, however stern and unbending, to yield to the dictates of justice, as he conceives it. His strength lies in his transparent sincerity and honesty of purpose, and his unflinching determination to practise what he preaches at all risks and at all hazards. His weakness lies in the fallacy of his supposition that the vast mass of the people can be trusted to imbibe his doctrines of peaceful aloofness from Government without trangressing the limits of law and order. Further, it lies in the inherent impracticableness of his concrete proposals, notably the boycotting of the courts by lawyers and of foreign goods by the public generally, and the withdrawing of boys and girls from schools and colleges. His proposal, which he puts in the forefront of his programme, that the reformed Legislative Councils should be boycotted, may succeed for a while and to some extent in certain quarters. But the vast bulk of the thinking public in India is not going to be guided in this matter by Mr. Gandhi's suicidal policy of not availing themselves of the opportunities which the Reform Act throws open to Indian talent and Indian capacity to further the growth of Parliamentary institutions in India, to have control of the administrative machine from within, and to utilise it to the best advantage for the welfare and uplift of their own countrymen, so as to justify and secure complete responsible government as rapidly as possible. Mr. Gandhi's programme and activity, therefore, need not cause undue anxiety and apprehension on the part of the authorities in India, and betray them into any indiscreet action of a repressive character. The fact that his programme has been endorsed by a majority vote of those who were present at the time of the voting at the Special Congress—for more than half of the registered delegates absented themselves when the vote was taken—does not necessarily mean that the people at large, or even the bulk of those who voted in his favour, are going to carry out his programme. Mr. Gandhi himself has enunciated the doctrine that a resolution of the Congress is not binding upon anyone whose conscience dictates that he should not abide by it. Many of the Extremist leaders are opposed to his programme, and it does not seem likely that they will, in spite of their own convictions, carry out that programme. Besides, that programme is opposed to the constitution of the Congress itself.

As for the Moderate Party—or the National Liberal Federation of India, as it has been recently known—I can say with confidence that there is not one among that vast body of the sober opinion in the country who favours Mr. Gandhi's movement. Several of them have publicly pointed out its unwisdom and absurdity. A capable writer in an open letter to Mr. Gandhi, published in *The Times of India*, points out that his policy of Non-Co-operation is impracticable and impossible of adoption, and observes: "Even for you it is impossible to follow. Are you prepared to avoid all Government concerns? You must cease to take advantage of post and telegraph services, law courts, and Government protection. You should have nothing to do with the Government officers. You should avoid Government coins and currency notes, and so on and so forth. Will all those who advocate the policy of Non-Co-operation observe it strictly? Then it will be a blessing to many a man, because debtors of such creditors can die in peace. Is it not idle to imagine that Government can be brought to its knees by the policy of Non-Co-operation?"

Thus there are many factors militating against the acceptance in practice of Mr. Gandhi's programme by the people at large. No useful purpose will, therefore, be served by exaggerating the importance of the resolution passed by the Congress, or imagining that something disastrous is going to take place in the near future as the result of it.

There is no doubt that it reveals a sulkiness which the Government can scarcely afford to disregard. But the task of wise statesmanship lies not in intensifying it by playing the agitator's game, but in diagnosing the real inwardness of this outward manifestation; and in doing so, the question which naturally suggests itself is: What is it that has created such a ferment in India latterly as to have made it possible for an idealist like Mr. Gandhi to succeed to the extent that he has? He first started his campaign of what he called Satyāgraha as a protest against that ill-advised measure known as the Rowlatt Act, which was in excess of the necessities of the case, going, as it did, in its drastic provisions even beyond the Irish Crimes Act, and which, although there was no urgency for it, the Government of India passed in the teeth of unanimous Indian non-official opposition to it in its Legislative Council. It is sometimes urged by some of the advocates of the measure that the opposition to it meant nothing else than sympathy with sedition and anarchism. That is an unjust accusation against a whole body of non-official Indians, nominated as well as elected, in the Government of India's legislature. Apart from the intrinsic demerits of the measure, what provoked and exasperated Indian feeling against it was the manner in which it was passed by the Government of India, betraying a spirit of riding rough-shod on Indian public opinion, as though it was absolutely unworthy of considerate treatment. Mr. Gandhi exploited public feeling on the subject to propagate his doctrine of "soul-force". The soil was ready for the seed. But he sowed the wind and reaped the whirlwind. He owned his mistake, however, and recoiled from it, but only when it was too late. Then came the Khilafat agitation. Mr. Gandhi, ever on the alert to take advantage of any general grievance, found in this an excellent opportunity to enlist Muslim opinion in favour of his favourite panacea. It is idle to deny that Muslim feeling in India has been embittered by the way in which Turkey has been dealt with by the Allied Powers in the Peace Treaty. There is a large body of thoughtful Indian opinion, however, both Muslim and non-Muslim, which is fully alive to the fact that the

Government of India and the Secretary of State pressed the Indian Muslim point of view with vigour and emphasis; and if the result has not been in accordance with Indian Muslim feeling in the matter, they cannot be held responsible for the ultimate decision, and there is no justification for carrying on a campaign of hatred against the Government of India and inflaming popular opinion against it. If this were the only handle available to those who are creating discontent in India, the agitation would have soon subsided. But unfortunately, there are other circumstances which have given rise to a general feeling of indignation against the Government of India and the British Government. The foremost among them is the Panjab affair. The attacks made on Mr. Montagu in the House of Commons and in a certain section of the British Press in connection with the Dyer debate; the vote of the House of Lords in favour of General Dyer; the funds raised in England and by certain European ladies and gentlemen in India to present a purse to General Dyer, and the considerable amount thus collected; the lavish praise bestowed by the British Cabinet on Sir Michael O'Dwyer, whose iron rule in the Panjab made the iron enter into the soul of the people in that province, and the failure of the Government of India to mete out adequate punishment to those Panjab officials who were guilty of excesses, and whose punishment was promised in the Cabinet's despatch on the Hunter Committee's Report—all these have produced a general feeling of resentment among all sections of the Indian public. Add to these the grievances of Indians in South Africa and East Africa, and the perpetuation of their unfair treatment based on racial grounds, and the tendency of the Government of India to provoke even Moderate public opinion against it by its arbitrary and despotic action now and again—and these, apart from the events in Egypt and in Ireland, will explain the unfortunate, but by no means unjustifiable, tension of feeling which has been gradually brought about among generally all classes of the people in India, and it is this state of things upon which Gandhism as well as Extremism work and thrive. And they will continue to thrive so long as this state of things is not radically remedied.

No radical remedy is perhaps possible unless a broad-minded statesman of the Canning-Ripon-Hardinge type is sent out to India to succeed Lord Chelmsford; and, further, unless the present Secretary of State for India, whose splendid work, against heavy odds and amidst tremendous difficulties, on behalf of India has won for him the esteem, regard and admiration of all those who are not blinded by prejudice, is given an absolutely free hand by the British Cabinet to improve the situation by pursuing a wise, courageous, and sympathetic policy, and, in regard to the status and treatment of Indians in the Dominions and Colonies, proposing a solution compatible with the rights of Indians as the King's equal subjects, which the British Cabinet should not hesitate to enforce in any part of the British Commonwealth in favour of India, which is now a member in her own right of the League of Nations. Until an atmosphere of genuine goodwill, fellow-feeling, sympathy and confidence in the British sense of fairness and justice in regard to Indian aspirations and demands is created, there is little hope, I fear, of a substantial improvement in the tone and mood of a large section of the Indian public.—*The Asiatic Review*, quoted in *The Servant of India.*

---

## CAMPAIGN AGAINST NON-CO-OPERATION

At the invitation of the Hon. Sir Dinshah Wacha a meeting of the Liberal Party in Bombay was held at the Cama Oriental Institute, on Saturday last, at 5 p.m., to discuss some features of the present political situation in the country, especially the question of Non-Co-operation, and to consider the best means of successfully organising and strengthening the forces of Liberalism. Sir Dinshah Wacha presided. Prominent amongst those present, besides the Chairman, were Sir Narayan Chandavarkar, the Hon. Mr. Gokuldas Parekh, the Hon. Mr. Purshottamdas Thakurdas, Messrs. K. Natarajan, N. V. Gokhale, Mirza Ali Mahomed Khan, V. P. Vaidya and others.

The Hon. Sir Dinshah opened the proceedings with a few preliminary remarks on the present political situation in the country. Sir Narayan Chandavarkar, Mr. K. Natarajan, among others took part in the proceedings. The meeting then passed the following resolution:

" (*a*) As in the opinion of this meeting the Non-Co-operation movement is dangerous to the best interests of the country, calculated to paralyse the people and lead not only to political dissentions but also social and domestic anarchy, and add to the existing forces which retard amity and union among the different castes and creeds of India, and as the movement will result in violence and consequentially set back the steady and stable progress of the country, this meeting resolves that the following steps be taken to educate public opinion against the movement, and point out to the masses in particular the dangers to which they are inevitably exposed by the movement.

" (i) Preparation and distribution of leaflets in the vernaculars, pointing out the reactionary nature and evil results of the movement.

" (ii) Formation of Committees for arranging lectures and meetings in different parts of the Presidency.

" (iii) Necessary action to be taken for giving a fair trial to the new Councils and enlightening the electors on the opportunity afforded to them by these Councils of speeding the cause of full Self-Government within the British Empire, and fostering the spirit of active and discriplined citizenship.

" (*b*) This meeting further resolves that a Committee consisting of the Hon. Sir D. E. Wacha, Sir Narayan Chandavarkar, Sir Chimanlal Setalvad, the Hon. Mr. G. K. Parekh, the Hon. Mr. Purshottamdas Thakurdas, Mr. K. Natarajan, Mr. N. V. Gokhale, Mr. J. R. Gharpure, Mr. J. K. Mehta, Mr. J. R. B. Jijibhoy, Mr. Uttamlal K. Trivedi, Mr. N. M. Joshi, Mr. M. D. Altekar, Mr. Sorabji E. Warden, Mr. S. S. Mehta, and Mr. D. G. Dalvi, with power to add, be appointed to devise measures and bring into operation the above resolution."

With a hearty vote of thanks to the Chair and to the Cama Oriental Institute, the meeting terminated.

# Dr. SAPRU ON NON-CO-OPERATION

The Hon. Dr. Tej Bahadur Sapru, in the course of an interview which a representative of the *Independent* had with him, stated his views on non-co-operation as follows:

My deliberate conviction is that the movement is not only impracticable but highly injurious to the interests of the country. In the first place, I feel that the programme of Non-Co-operation as laid down by Mr. Gandhi is not capable of fulfilment. In the next place, I think that even if it were capable of realisation it would give rise to a spirit which, to my mind will be wholly detrimental to the further development of the country. Nor I do look upon it as at all likely that the Turkish Treaty can be modified by the present movement. For one man who will enter upon the campaign of Non-Co-operation in a spirit of meek suffering, there will be five who will be moved by racial considerations and racial hatred. Once it is recognised that it is a weapon which we can use for political purposes, you cannot draw the line and you do not know where to stop.

I am not aware, that any such movement has achieved a great end anywhere in recent times. I do not think that even its supporters can justify it by analogy to Sinn Fein in Ireland, because the latter is avowedly both militant and aggressive, and in no sense can you call it a movement of Non-Co-operation.

When I talk of it as impracticable, I have in view the suggestion that paid officers should withdraw from their practice. At the Conference I said that it was obviously unfair and unjust to ask subordinate officers getting small salaries to resign their posts when it was quite clear to my mind that men in the position of Judges in High Courts or other high Indian officials could not be expected to throw up their appointments.

If you remove your boys from Government schools, whom do you hurt but yourselves and your boys? It is like cutting the nose to spite the face. As for the refusal to pay income-tax and land revenue, I should feel very much interested to see how many of the Zamindars and the Talukdars in these Provinces, are prepared at the next collection time to say "no" to the tax gatherer.

And then to complete your programme, you must ask the Police and the Army to resign their offices. I refuse to believe that this will happen. But assuming it does, can you seriously contemplate a contingency like that with equanimity—I would not call it Non-Co-operation. I should be frank, and say it was a revolution."

Questioned with regard to what he thought of the Council boycott, Dr. Sapru said: "So far as the party to which I belong is concerned, it is not going to boycott the Councils. And from all that I know of the Zamindars, I do not think that they too are going to boycott the Councils. As for the party to which you belong, you know as well as I that you are hopelessly divided on this question. I do not think that by boycotting the Councils we can get better Councils or full self-government at once."

Dr. Sapru further stated: "My belief is that the present temper is only a passing phase. A combination of circumstances may be referred to to explain it, and no party in India can always live or carry on work in this state of tension."

---

[From *New India*, September and October, 1920]

## NON-CO-OPERATION

THE Non-Co-operation Movement is spreading, and it looks as though Mr. Gandhi would soon be a "back number". His conceded word, "gradual," which took all the vim out of the order to withdraw children from schools and lawyers from Courts, is being contemptuously struck out of the Congress resolution; the Muslim League led the way, and others are following. The Sylhet Conference, of one thousand delegates and three thousand visitors, struck it out, and went further along the Non-Co-operation road. It passed resolutions:

(1) To refuse to take service under European planters and merchants and gradual withdrawal of those already under such service. (2) Non-acceptance of briefs by lawyers from such planters and merchants. (3) Refusal on the part of the people to grant fresh leases or to renew old ones. (4) To abstain from attending any function in which such non-official Europeans are invited.

The Conference further calls on Indians:

(1) To oppose Imperial Preference and encourage the trade in Indian raw materials with friendly countries outside the British Empire. (2) To boycott all articles of luxury imported from the United Kingdom and to restrict the use of other foreign goods within such limits as the insufficiency of indigenous production imperatively necessitates. (3) To withdraw all Indian money so far as possible from British banks in India, and patronise for purposes of foreign trade non-British banks. (4) To start Trade Unions with a view to the organisation and education of the Indian labouring classes of their right and liberties. (5) To gradually withdraw Indian labour from all industrial concerns supported by British capital or under British management. (6) To demand the immediate repeal of all legislation dealing with labour in India which militates against the elementary freedom of man in regard to the disposal of his labour. (7) To organise home industries in every village with a view to meet the essential necessaries of life.

It will be seen that these resolutions are drawn partly from Mr. Pal's amendment. No. 2 is less wild than the general boycott forced on Mr. Gandhi, and No. 3 introduces an "as far as possible"; one would like to know how any foreign trade (which may be left) can patronise non-British Banks? Can drafts on Indian Banks be obtained in London? We have tried to obtain them, and have failed.

In "Instruction for Non-Co-operation," a draft not yet confirmed, the light-hearted way in which big schemes are recommended strikes us with consternation. "To take steps for the establishment of National Universities." Have the drafters any idea of what this means in men, money, and continuous labour? Business relations are to be discontinued "as far as may be," with all who do not obey the Conference. Is it permissible to ask who is going to employ all the labour withdrawn from British-controlled concerns? Who will feed and house the wives and children of the unemployed labourers? If Assam carries out the resolution it may drive the British into bankruptcy, but it will also drive the labouring population into starvation. Industry cannot suddenly be dislocated without causing untold misery.

Among the many letters in the current *Hindu* are three on Mr. Sastri's disallowed resolution. It does not seem to strike the writers that in the Council as it is, there is an official majority, presided over by the Governor-General; in the Legislature as it will be, there are two houses, both with elected majorities, and the Governor-General will no longer preside. This profound difference in the Central Government cripples the power of the Governor-General, and he will be gradually forced into the position of a constitutional monarch. How quickly this is done depends on the people, not on the Government.

Some of the letter-writers counsel delay. One, who quite logically points out that if the resolution is a mandate, it should be a mandate throughout, and there should be no picking and choosing between its clauses, asks:

> What will these teeming millions of India do, when vakils cease their practice and students abstain from going to Colleges and nothing is done in Councils? The question of poverty that is affecting the peasant, the teacher, the Government servant and the lawyer, and further dislocation of appointments and uncertainty of life as a result of the adoption of this scheme of Non-Co-operation, are the important factors that have been doing much to weaken the Congress faith and to adopt it whole heartedly.

(The last six words are unintelligible in view of the context.) The "springing up of National schools," spoken of by Mr. Gandhi, is eminently desirable, but unhappily they do not spring up spontaneously. Who is going to build schools, even of wattle and thatch, to accommodate the millions of scholars, and who is going to pay the teachers? Mr. Gandhi says that the present teachers may go on in the National schools, but will their salaries go on? The *practical* idealist, who has tried to bring some of his ideals into human life, stands aghast at the light way in which the non-practical idealist spreads abroad his schemes in the mental atmosphere, with never a thought as to how they can be brought down to the physical. The worst of this policy is that it enthuses the people, who take it for granted that their leaders will carry it out, and they will not attend to such terrestrial matters as sending good men to the Councils.

Non-Co-operation has even entered the non-Brahmana camp, and caused a split, so that while we have Sir Theagaraya Chetti throwing himself at the feet of the Government, eager for boons, we have a non-Brahmana Conference adopting Non-Co-operation and bidding candidates withdraw from election. Many strange results will come from this explosive firework. It reminds one of the startling species which run along the ground and explode at intervals.

---

## THE PRACTICAL FRUITS OF NON-CO-OPERATION

THE final test of every movement, "the verdict of history," to use the Viceroy's quotation, is to be found in the saying, "by their fruits ye shall know them," and the movement of Non-Co-operation can claim no exemption from the application of this sound test. The stage of finality is as yet perhaps far off; but the movement has been in active progress for nearly two months, and the mandate of the Special Congress was given three weeks ago. So far, the practical results of launching this fateful movement have not been such as to permit Mr. Gandhi and his followers to congratulate themselves thereon. A certain number of Congressmen in every Province have, out of a mistaken sense of duty, withdrawn their candidatures to the Councils. A few, but only a very few, lawyers have suspended practice; on a generous estimate about fifty children have been withdrawn from schools; one or two Arbitration Courts have also been set up. And need we point to the sad but true experience, that in this country enthusiasm for any cause is unsustained and, after a fine outburst, is succeeded by a few flickers before final extinction? It may be urged that the resolution is advisory, not mandatory; that the only part of the resolution immediately operative is that relating to the boycott of Councils, while other clauses are qualified by the word "gradual"; and that, in any case, the Report of the Sub-Committee which has drawn up the instructions, will only be considered by the All-India Congress Committee on Saturday next. Those who have chosen this path, walk on the exceedingly "thin ice" of casuistry. The mandatory theory dates only from the Amritsar Congress, whose resolution on the Reforms, as we pointed out a few days ago, went no further than a bare expression of opinion on their "inadequate, unsatisfactory and disappointing" nature, and a recommendation that they should be worked in order to hasten the advent of full Responsible Government. Again, there was absolutely no necessity for a Sub-Committee to draw up instructions, or for the All-India Congress Committee to meet now, if the sense of loyalty, mistaken and regrettable as it is, had been a hearty one. Let us frankly acknowledge that to a majority of those who have obeyed the Congress in the matter of Council elections, the expenditure of money and the risks of failure which have been considerably increased by the resolution of the Congress have provided a convenient means of making a virtue of necessity. The elections were to be run, according to the original intentions of the Nationalists, on the party basis of "Congressmen" versus the "rebels". No other issue having been placed by them before the electorates, the Special Congress has removed the only plank on which erstwhile Congressmen could stand. Their practical difficulties in seeking the suffrages of the voters, with the Liberal candidates equally busy, and Mr. Gandhi's followers not less so in carrying out the injunctions of the Congress to boycott the polling booths, would have been so great that we are not surprised that the Congress party has decided with a few exceptions to tread the path of prudence and apparent consistency.

But leaving the subject of the Councils alone, how far has the rest of the programme of Non-Co-operation been, or is likely to be, carried? We will presume that the Non-Co-operators are favoured with continued good luck on their perilous voyage through an uncharted sea. The Government, let us hope, will keep a wise and cool head and no untoward happenings, no riots or bloodshed, will mar the non-violent character of the movement. But even under the most auspicious circumstances, what is it that they hope to achieve? The one and only object of the movement is to secure the paralysis of the Government. Now, paralysis is an affection of the motor or sensory nerves of an organism. If there had been an immediate and wholesale withdrawal of boys (and girls) from schools and colleges and a stoppage on the same scale of practice by lawyers, we admit that a "moral effect," a warning twitch of the nerves of the administration might have been produced. But the "sensory nerves" of the Government would have been touched only by resignations from the police and military, and the "motor nerves" by resignations from Government posts and by the non-payment of taxes. Nothing of the sort, however, is even intended at this stage. Mr. Gandhi and his followers, it is said, are not unreasonable men. National educational institutions, Arbitration Courts and handloom weaving will precede the several forms of boycott prescribed. The Non-Co-operators have throughout repudiated the idea that the movement is one of negation. Within the cordon of negation, will be activity which is to bring us Swarâj in a year or two. A movement for nationalising education, or for encouraging Swadeshism, or for the decrease of litigation would have been welcomed as strengthening their respective aspects of National life. But not at the expense of stifling all political life and not for the purpose of paralysing the administration. Could the movement on its purely constructional side have brought us Swarāj within the period guaranteed? But at all events, the country would have been unanimous in diverting a part of its energies into these useful channels of activity. What Non-Co-operation has really done is to paralyse our public life at a critical period. Before the Special Congress met, there was some talk of collecting funds for legal proceedings against some of the arch-offenders in the Panjab. That idea seems to have been effectively killed. Both the Turkish Treaty and the Panjab have steadily receded into the background. Mr. Gandhi and his followers have taken up the programme of the Special Congress, with what results we have already stated. They may perhaps succeed in inducing a fair proportion of the voters to refrain from voting. But while it will not bring on paralysis of the Government, it will be used as an effective argument against the extension of the franchise in later years. Those who are for "Non-Co-operation in principle alone" are busy marshalling their forces to rescind the Special Congress decision at Nagpur. Time and energy which should be utilised for political propaganda for the country's needs are being given to petty party ends. To the Liberals and National Home Rulers alone has been left a task which is great enough and heavy enough for all to bear. With the forces of reaction are most unfortunately allied in purpose, though not in intention, the Non-Co-operators, while at a critical moment, the Nationalists have gone out of the struggle. Such, to our minds, are the fruits both materialised and prospective, of the Non-Co-operation movement.

## CONGRESS SUB-COMMITTEE

THE Report of the Sub-Committee appointed by the All-India Congress Committee to make a draft of Instructions to Non-Co-operators will come on many like a douche of cold water, so severely practical is it, so intolerant of evasions and subterfuges.

After reciting the various ways in which the first step is to be carried out, it asserts that the Congress " has approved of Mr. Gandhi's full programme of progressive, non-violent Non-Co-operation, but has adopted for immediate use the items in the first stage only ". The remaining three stages will be set going in due course. Lala Lajpat Rai has challenged this remark, but it is literally accurate. The Congress passed the whole Resolution, as printed for the Subjects' Committee and as in the Agenda. The Resolution included in one of its paragraphs Mr. Gandhi's programme, and it therefore forms part of the Resolution supposed to be binding on all who voted for it. It may be that Lala Lajpat Rai did not read it, and that Mr. Patel did not read it. But for that lapse none is to blame but themselves. Lalaji is quite wrong in saying that the Special Congress did not approve Mr. Gandhi's full programme. The Congress passed the resolution and it was printed for the Subjects' Committee and read in Congress. If people are so careless, or so excited, as not to know what they are voting for, they must none the less be held to be responsible for their votes. If anyone has a right to cancel parts of a resolution passed by the Congress, because he does not like it, resolutions would undergo serious mutilations. The poll was taken on the morning after the debate, so people who voted carelessly in the show of hands had time to acquaint themselves with the resolution before they went to the poll. We are told that the Congress expresses the voice of the Nation and that its resolutions are binding. What right has Mr. Patel to cut out this part of the National Will expressed in the Congress?

It is quite true that the Congress did not discuss this part of the Resolution but no one prevented discussion, and there the resolution stands, including the second, third and fourth steps of Mr. Gandhi's programme. Congress passed them and thereby approved them. Non-Co-operators, having triumphed at the Congress, should surely not reject their sweeping success, and come down towards the position of the vanquished, step by step.

Even if the All-India Congress Committee, wishing to run with the hare and hunt with the hounds, deletes the paragraph in the Report, they cannot delete the corresponding part of the Resolution, embodied in the Congress Report, for that would be to falsify the record—an impossible thing for honourable men. We fear they must shoulder the result of their carelessness. To show any hesitation will be to break the Hindu-Musalman Entente, for the Musalmans, at least, know what they are doing.

We may note here that while Lalaji and Mr. Patel sin in one direction, by omitting part of the Congress Resolution, the whole Sub-Committee sin in another, by inserting in another part of the Resolution what is not there. The Resolution, sub-clause (*f*), proposes the boycotting of recruiting for service in Mesopotamia, and the Committee inserts as though it were part of the Resolution "(meaning Turkish Dominions as on the outbreak of the War)"; nothing happened to imply any such meaning.

On the boycott of titles, the Report says that it is very easy, and that all who voted for the resolution and have titles "are naturally expected immediately to surrender them". That natural expectation, we fancy, is going to be disappointed.

Workers in every district, taluq, and town are to compile lists of all title-holders and holders of honorary offices, and a deputation is to wait on them and beg them politely to surrender these.

Mr. Patel goes even further, and if his suggestions are carried out, the lives of Co-operators will be made a burden to them by deputations.

Deputations to right of them,
Deputations to left of them,
Deputations behind them,
(Will) volley and thunder.

Whenever there are Levees, or Darbars, or any function in honour of, or given by, an official, Deputations and public meetings are to be let loose on every guest. Does it not strike Mr. Patel that the guests may not co-operate with deputations by receiving them ?

When the deputations have done their full work, names are to be sent up for publication by the Central Committee; what will happen to the obstinate ones is left to the imagination. They will form a black list, and will probably be subjected to the terrors of the social boycott. As, however, they are likely far to outnumber the obedient, they can have their own parties and other functions, and can ostracise the obedient. The mutual boycott will not increase the happiness of Society, but what of that? "Gradually" all these foolish plans will fail and disappear, and Society will go on again on its old lines.

## NON-CO-OPERATION

It is perhaps not strange that the movement for Non-Co-operation, which threatens the peace and prosperity of India at the very moment when large powers are passing out of the hands of the Bureaucracy into those of the people, attracts persons who have evidently never troubled themselves to read the Reform Act; for it would be cruel to suppose that they deliberately invent the false statements they put forward in the press, as reasons for supporting this destructive movement. Their reasons echo the untrue statements which have been propagated from so-called Nationalist platforms, in the effort of the orators to discredit the Moderates by representing them as supporting a useless measure, in order to secure seats in the Councils and to please the Government.

An illustration of the extraordinary recklessness with which untrue statements are unwittingly made is found in a letter which appears in *The Hindu*. The writer says :

> The most important subjects, on which the life and progress of a nation depend, are reserved, and remain the exclusive monopoly of the bureaucracy. Our representatives in the Councils are, therefore, doomed to make as ever unheeded protests.

Is this statement true? Is Agriculture a reserved subject? Is Sanitation a reserved subject? Is Local Government a reserved subject? Is Education a reserved subject?—to take only four. Are not these the most vital subjects "on which the life and progress of a Nation depend"? Land Revenue, also most important, is to be placed on a statutory basis and then handed over; that is a great omission in the present Act, but that does not make true the sweeping statement that "the most important subjects, on which the life and progress of a Nation depend, are reserved". The fact is the very opposite. It is most of the vital subjects that are transferred. The power to deal with these is given to Ministers, and Councillors may not vote against the Ministers' decision. If the elected majority stand firmly by their Ministers, the latter *must* carry the day. "But the Governor can veto a Bill," says the supporter of Non-Co-operation. True, for he exercises the Royal Prerogative, and the King can veto a Bill by refusing to sign it. Suppose he does. The Ministers resign, and the majority supports them. The Governor dissolves the Council. The electorate returns the same majority. The same Bill is again passed, and as the Report remarked, it is hoped that the Governor will adapt himself to the view on which the dissolution took place. Is it said that the Council and the electorate will not stand firm? Then they are not fit for Self-Government. Believing that they are fit for it, we believe that they will stand firm and will win their liberty by fighting for it against a rebellious Governor, as England won hers by fighting against rebellious Kings. Liberty cannot be wisely given; only the power to take it should be given, for if it is treated as a boon from a superior to an inferior, it would not be kept; "eternal vigilance is the price of liberty". When the power to win it, as a Right acknowledged by the rulers, is placed within the hands of the people, the struggle develops the strength which ensures the keeping of the precious Right that they have won. If it be true that "Nations by themselves are made," then India must make herself and not be made by England. England has done what she could, but India must take the liberty placed within her reach.

A Bill amending the present Acts affecting Local Government and making it complete, without any room for interference by the Civilians, is of the first necessity. The successful carrying out of Education, Sanitation, and Agricultural improvement can only be done effectually through the Panchayat, the Taluq Board and the District Board. Only in this way will the people govern themselves through their elected representatives in all the matters which touch their daily life and prosperity. It was this democratic local self-government which carried India rich and prosperous through all the wars and invasions that she suffered, like all the contemporary countries from 3000 B.C. to A.D. 1858. It is the recovery of this that she needs for the renewal of prosperity, and she must do it for herself; how badly it is done for her by Westerners, however well-meaning, is seen in the Panchayat Act, which deprives village women of their immemorial right to vote when duly qualified. But only by voting for capable Indians as members of the Councils can real Local Government be won, and with it the local control of education, sanitation, agricultural improvement, and the amenities and conveniences of well-ordered village life. Mr. Gandhi asks us to boycott the Councils, and thus helps to fill them with men who will be reactionary and indifferent to the lot of the villagers. If Liberals, National Home Rulers and Nationalists do not vote, who will fill the Councils? The Europeans, the Christians, and the Johukum Hindus and Musalmans. Mr. Gandhi would persuade men to leave the country in their hands for the next three years, while the Reformers sit outside trying to paralyse the Government.

Our letter-writer wants all kinds of assurances that the bureaucracy will not flout the Nation's opinions and feelings. Who is to give them? Surely not the bureaucracy? It is the Nation's business to see that it is not flouted. Government can go on despite meetings and protests, but it could not go on against the strong and determined assertion in the Legislative Council of those opinions and feelings. Non-Co-operators always refer to what has been done by an official majority, as though the same thing would happen with an elected majority! They assert that things which are different will have the same result.

Why should the same people outside the Council be more powerful than they would be within the Councils? we may venture to ask. Our writer speaks of "mere academic discussions" in Councils. But why should discussions in a law-making assembly be academic? One could imagine that Non-Co-operators are political Rip van Winkels, prattling about conditions long left behind. We are told that "India"—consisting of 1,826 Indians out of nearly 6,000—resolved to boycott the Councils. "India's" resolution will be clearer, when the six million voters have voted or refused to vote.

It makes one despair to read:

> Except the extension of franchise and allowing more men to vote, and to sit in the Council to play at holding discussions and passing resolutions which can never become laws unless the bureaucracy God-fathered them, the Reforms have done nothing more.

The bureaucracy have absolutely nothing to do with the laws passed on transferred subjects.

Another writer says that the passage of the resolution of Non-Co-operation was due to disgust at the failure of almost every one of the attempts to get redress, and to the growth of National self-respect. But the failure was *before* the new powers were available. He wants means other than "the already much-tried methods". He has them in Councils with an overwhelming elected majority. But instead of at least giving them a trial, and bestirring himself to send the best men to do as men like them have done in other countries, he goes off after a Will-o'-the-Wisp that can do nothing at all.

Much is said about the self-sacrifice implied in boycotting the Councils, and the self-seeking connoted by going into them. The truth is the opposite. A lawyer with a big practice has to impoverish himself by giving it up, in order to give his time to the service of his country, the most thankless of all tasks. It is he who makes the real sacrifice and is the true patriot. This is coolly ignored, and persons who sacrifice nothing hoot at him. Why do not all the students who shout for Non-Co-operation sacrifice their careers by leaving their Colleges?

---

## NON-CO-OPERATION IN PRACTICE

UNDER this heading, *The Bombay Chronicle* of the 9th October, which only reached us yesterday too late for comment, has given what it calls "an official account of the proceedings of the All-India Congress Committee" on October 2. We reprint it to-day.

The second clause is surprising, as the Nagpur Reception Committee, after being granted the delay it asked for, elected the President without waiting for the votes of Bombay, the United Provinces and Burma. If these were all given to one of the other names proposed, it would still leave Mr. Vijiaraghavachariar with a majority of two, so that the absence of those votes does not affect the result.

The third resolution established the All-India Lokomanya Tilak Memorial Fund. We trust the memorial chosen will be one to which all can contribute, and not a mere party movement.

The fourth resolution is the vital one. The preamble is omitted. The Boycott of Councils follows the Draft of the Sub-Committee, save the opening words down to "shunned," so that the Government is not branded as unrighteous. (See *N. I.*, September 30, for Draft.) A new clause on the Boycott of Government Functions follows, advising pressure by deputations and public meetings to be put on all who attend. This advice is most regrettable; the interference with the liberty of individuals to order their own lives is tyrannical and impertinent, and will induce bitter feelings everywhere, shattering the social feeling on which so much happiness depends. The clause on Boycott of Schools and Colleges has been redrafted, Mr. Gandhi's explanation of "gradual"—blessed word—is deleted. A National Institution is defined as one that does not receive any aid from Government, is not controlled nor inspected by Government, and is not affiliated to any University. Boycott of Law Courts is redrafted, and the hortatory part removed. The Committee was evidently in a severely practical mood. People who are induced to go to an Arbitration Court are to be socially boycotted if they do not abide by the award; moral, do not go. The Boycott of Councils is to be vigorously pressed, and electors are to be urged to sign a form stating that they do not wish to be represented. Those who sign it, having betrayed their trust, must not complain if bad laws are passed; they are strengthening autocracy and bureaucracy, are casting away the citizenship won after years of struggle by patriotic men, and are refusing to do their duty to their Motherland. In some free countries men who thus neglect their duty are fined, as having committed an offence against their native land. Attempts are to be made to prevent "labour, etc." from going to Mesopotamia. The Committee was very careful to protect itself; the "etc." covers military recruiting, but that, plainly stated, might be dangerous. Boycott of foreign goods was narrowed down to dispensing with luxuries. As a mere matter of honesty, has the Committee any right to deal with a Congress resolution as it pleases, whittling it down as in these last two cases? One can respect the self-denial and the courage of honest Non-Co-operators, who carry out what they pretend; but it is difficult not to feel contempt for those who impose heavy burdens on others, and whittle away matters which would inconvenience themselves. Posing as heroes before the Nation at a Congress amid vociferous applause, hooting those who venture to point out the impossibility of carrying out the resolution, and then carefully eliminating the inconvenient details so that it may not press on themselves too hardly, is a hypocrisy which poisons the life-blood of a Nation.

Of course, Mr. Gandhi's favourite spinning-wheel was approved; a Swarāj fund is to be started, and volunteer corps are to be trained.

Lastly, the Committee thanked Colonel Wedgwood, M.P., and Mr. Ben Spoor, M. P., and welcomed them to the country, where they will have the pleasure of seeing, at the Congress, their advice set at nought.

It is useless to protest merely, we must work to stop this fatal movement, which would destroy education, leave the people in their poverty and misery, and establish an intolerable tyranny. Happily they cannot keep the Councils empty, and these will be able to work at useful legislation while the Non-Co-operators work in a way that will reduce the country to anarchy and lay it open to foreign invasion as well as to internal disorder. Let all good citizens unite in this moment of the Nation's peril, and prevent the National suicide to which Non-Co-operation is impelling the Motherland.

## HUMAN RIGHTS

THE destruction of the Rights of the Nation is going on at the hands of Mr. Gandhi and his followers to a much greater extent than happened in the days of the unrestricted power of the bureaucracy. They are already establishing a tyranny which gives us a foretaste of what we shall have to endure if they succeed in their present effort to paralyse the Government. The disgraceful scenes which marred the dignity of the Calcutta Congress, when Mrs. Besant was howled down and only permitted to speak by grace of Mr. Gandhi, and where Mr. Jamnadas Dwarkadas spoke amid a hurricane of yells, Mr. Gandhi not intervening and the President being unable to control the audience, are repeated in miniature in smaller gatherings. In Moradabad, the Calcutta scene was repeated with the significant change that even Mr. Gandhi could not obtain order speaking through his deputy, and only after the President said that he would leave the chair unless the audience gave the speaker—Mr. Banki Bihari Varma—a hearing, did the crowd settle down, after "several minutes" of uproar.

If the Government silenced every speaker who spoke against it, the sky would be rent with shouts of the tyranny of the Government. What is the difference in principle between such action by the Government, and the action of the crowds all over India who silence, by howling them down, speakers with whom they disagree? The only tyranny now in India is the tyranny of the crowd, so far as free speech is concerned. The Government hears itself called "inhuman," "cruel," "unrighteous," and very sensibly only smiles at the epithet-hurlers, and goes quietly on its way, unheeding. No Executive action is anywhere taken against Free Speech, but the followers of the Dictator take up the rôle the bureaucracy has surrendered, and enforce their will with far more rudeness than was shown by the bureaucracy of the past.

There is no Right of Free Speech now in India; only that may be spoken from the platform which agrees with the views of the new "spiritualised democracy". The old courtesy, the old kindliness, the old self-control, so characteristic of Indians, have now disappeared; they are as rough as a western crowd; and it will not be long before violent Non-Co-operation against speech becomes violent Non-Co-operation against the speakers, and against all who do not share in the momentary passions of the crowd. Mr. Gandhi, of course, will disclaim all responsibility, pleading that he exhorted people not to use violence. When the course advised inevitably leads to violence, it is idle to seek shelter from responsibility in words.

Just as the Non-Co-operation movement is destroying the Right of Free Speech for adults, so is it seeking to deprive the helpless children of the Nation from their primary natural Right to Education. Happily, the parents who shout for Non-Co-operation and howl down even a proposal to amend the egregious Calcutta resolution, are themselves Co-operators with Government by not withdrawing their children from school; they thus save their children at the cost of their consistency—a very fortunate thing.

The Right of Representation is sought to be destroyed, although the National Congress has been demanding it since 1885. People are to be persuaded to renounce their Duty of Citizenship, and their Right to share in the Government of their own country. They are to be pestered to give up their Right as free men by deputations and public meetings which seek to terrorise them, and we read about a picket at every polling-booth to dissuade voters from exercising their Right to vote.

The Right to protection from violence is also assailed; if a man robs, assaults, even murders, there is to be no resort to the King's Courts. Law Courts are to be boycotted, so the injured must not even give evidence against the injurer.

Such is the crusade against Human Rights, initiated by Mr. Gandhi. It leads straight to anarchy. We have not mentioned other items of his programme, such as the proposed call to the police and soldiers to resign. He would thus leave our frontiers undefended—perhaps sharing his friend Shaukat Ali's view that the Afghans are fine fellows and good Muslims—as well as our towns at the mercy of the predatory classes. If he succeeds, we shall pass into an anarchy from which only a military Dictator will be able to rescue us, and all the fair hopes of Liberty which have begun to flower will be destroyed. Mr. Gandhi is beginning to justify the views of Lord Sydenham and other enemies of Indian Liberty—as the non-Brahmanas of Madras are also doing on other lines—by stirring up the passions of the people at this critical moment, when all thoughts should be centred on sending the best men to the Reformed Councils, and on the work they have to do. Will not India awaken to her danger ere it be too late, and turn from the downward path into which her feet have strayed ?

---

## WILD TALK

THE Aligarh bubble has burst, and the disturbers of the peace are outside the College buildings without the use of force, thanks to the firmness of the Trustees and the tact of the District Magistrate, who was appealed to when the Trustees heard that the property they held for the Muhammadan community was being injured by Mr. Muhammad Ali and his rebellious students. The preceding talk was wild enough. Mr. Muhammad Ali was doing "God's work," and as he was "acting in obedience to His commandments" he could not accede to the request of the Trustees to vacate the building. Was it not Professor Huxley who remarked that some people talked of the Deity as though they were in the habit of taking tea with Him ? Some Non-Co-operators take much the same tone. When, however, the District Magistrate, after providing facilities for the transport of persons and luggage, quietly suggested to Mr. Muhammad Ali that he should withdraw and take his boys with him, "God's work" faded away, and Mr. Muhammad Ali had the good sense to co-operate with the Government and to leave the Boarding House with his young rebels. It would probably be too much to hope that this humiliation will teach young men not to put themselves into a position which their leaders vacate as soon as an official appears. "Put not your trust in Non-Co-operators, for there is no help in them." Theirs is only, we are thankful to say, lip-courage—wild words in plenty, but no steadfastness. They lead boys to destruction, but cannot protect them.

The new University was to be opened on October 29th, but no news of it had arrived on November 2nd, the time of writing this article. There were meetings, in which prayers and denunciations were sandwiched, so as to use religion to excite passion. After saying his prayers, on October 28th, Mr. Hasrat Mohani advocated turning the Aligarh buildings into a University, "sticking to the buildings at all costs". On the 31st, there was no University, but a quiet surrender of the buildings, as described above. Mr. Mohani further stated that Trustees voting against Non-Co-operation "were no longer Muslims, and *ipso facto* ceased to be Trustees and their order was not binding". Who gave this peremptory gentleman the right to expel his fellow-Muslims? On October 29th, addressing a crowd of some five thousand people, Mr. Muhammad Ali condemned the Trustees; the telegram says that cries were heard, "Kill Ziauddin". Will Mr. Muhammad Ali hold himself guiltless of murder, if the passions he raised result in such killing? The circular convening the abortive meeting to found the New University asked the people to come with "excessive passionate enthusiasm"; "self-controlled deep enthusiasm" is a better gift to lay on the Altar of the Motherland. The other destroys, it does not build; it shouts, but does not create wise action.

Another illustration of wild talk is the starting of "National Universities". The new Muslim University, which was to have been started on October 29th, was apparently based on nothing more substantial than the hopes of the Destroying Trio that they would gain possession of the College lands and buildings by seizing them and refusing to vacate. That violent seizure of the property held in trust for Islam by a body of devoted Musalmans was defeated by their brave resistance, so University No. 1 has not materialised. University No. 2 was to be opened at Allahabad, on November 1st; Pandit Motilal Nehru offered his beautiful house for the purpose, but a building does not make a University. No staff was engaged, no laboratories fitted up, nothing in fact was there except a fine house, well furnished as a dwelling-house. To speak of opening a University under these circumstances is characteristic of the Non-Co-operation movement; it is all talk, intended to excite the imagination of the people and to blind them to the fact that nothing is being *done*; it is all mere bluff.

The propaganda of destruction is next to assail Benares Hindu University; Mr. Gandhi writes that he has "no hesitation in advising immediate destruction of these institutions at all cost". Why? The Central Hindu College and School never received a rupee from the Government; the Government now contributes a lakh annually to the University, but attaches no conditions to it. What has it done that it should be destroyed? It was built up by sacrifice, devotion and love for the service of the Motherland. Why do the destroyers seek to ruin the work of others, to which they have contributed nothing?

And why does not Mr. Gandhi build new schools and colleges for the youths to whom he has taught disobedience to parents and teachers? It will be interesting to see his management, and the education which will justify his contempt for the education which trained Gokhale and Pherozeshah Mehta, and Ranade, and Telang, and Tyabji, and Wacha, and, later, Srinivasa Sastri, and Tej Bahadur Sapru, and C. Y. Chintamani, and C. P. Ramaswami Aiyar, to name but a few of the hundreds who made the Congress what it was. Imperfect and defective as it is, it need not be ashamed of its products, and the hatred shown by men like O'Dwyer for the educated classes is its highest testimonial. Mr. Gandhi himself is its product, though we admit he has not learnt its lesson of liberty and tolerance. It needs mending, not ending, but Mr. Gandhi has done naught to mend it.

Mr. Gandhi's latest complaint against the Government is that its officials eat pork and beef, and thus wound the deepest feelings of Musalmans and Hindus. But this is not a sudden offence. Why did Mr. Gandhi accept a Kaiser-i-Hind medal from a Government eating such unpleasant food, and why did he recruit for it so vigorously? And what about the Hindu-Muslim entente? The Musalmans are beef-eaters quite as much as the Englishmen, and should therefore be similarly loathed.

Why is Mr. Gandhi now seeking to destroy educational institutions dear to Musalman and Hindu respectively, in which each feels a patriotic pride? Why does he try to set Hindus against Musalmans by writing so offensively of beef-eaters? *Because his Non-Co-operation has failed, and he is trying to cover his defeat.* Pandit Motilal Nehru is the solitary leading lawyer who has resigned a lucrative practice. How many titleholders have resigned? How many Government honorary servants? How many have boycotted the Councils? See the United Provinces;

*The Leader* gives the figures: there are 89 general seats in the U.P., and 301 candidates; there is an average of 4 candidates to each non-Muslim seat, and 73 Muslims contest 29 seats. In the Legislative Assembly, the U.P. has 15 seats and 52 candidates dispute them; there are 5 seats in the Council of State, and 12 candidates struggle for them. Five months have passed since the Allahabad Khilafat Conference, and his *first step* has made no way in the country. Having failed abjectly with the mature, he turns to the immature, and is carrying on a desperate campaign to ruin their future lives.

Under these circumstances, may we not implore the Government of India and the Provincial Governments not to be provoked into taking any notice of him? He is obviously trying to provoke them into arresting him, by saying one outrageous thing after another, for that would make him a martyr, and the failure of his movement would be said to be due to his arrest. The failure is inevitable, if he be left alone. He is dividing his own followers by his wild talk, is alienating all pious Muslims by teaching rebellion to their sons and wards and driving them out of the colleges in which their parents have placed them. He reviles all beef-eaters, and thus angers Musalmans. He gives a pledge to leave students alone, and breaks it. He makes promises he does not fulfil. He threatens the peace of the country by talking of "when we take up swords". Leave him alone, we beg, for he is discrediting himself and ruining his movement. Let not any Government fall into the trap he baits so cleverly, for that will save him and perpetuate his influence. Left alone, he will entangle himself in his innumerable letters and speeches, and his whole movement will come to an inglorious end. Let not the bathos which will kill it be changed by repression into tragedy.

---

## THE DESTROYERS

By Annie Besant

One by one the things for which Indians have struggled and sacrificed are being taken away from them and destroyed under the fair pretext of patriotism and "higher politics". The meaning of "higher politics" has not been vouchsafed to us, but its effects are only too clearly seen, and they are effects which will long outlast their creators. For they are corrupting the youth of India at the critical age at which character, slowly formed during school, is crystallising into definite shape, and the manhood of the elder collegians and young graduates is receiving a twist which will not be wholly straightened out in this life, and the results of which will be seen when power passes into their hands.

The boyhood and youth of India at the end of the last century were too quiet, too submissive, too indifferent for the most part to games and exercise. In the College and School of Aligarh, in the Central Hindu College and School of Benares a new type was developed, frank, manly, brave, courteous, full of love of, pride in, country, but withal obedient to rightful authority, healthy and self-controlled. The "Old Boys" of both Aligarh and Benares are men of whom any country might be proud. Their contemporaries in Government Colleges were also strongly affected by the influences of the time, and, speaking roughly, the men from about 30 to 50 years of age are the strength and the hope of the country. They are brave without arrogance, strong without insolence, religious without intolerance, courteous without servility. Many of the Professors in Government Colleges were Englishmen of the best type, who loved and respected their students, who in return rendered them love and respect.

All went well and the popular movement—largely accelerated by the proclamations of the Allies during the War, proclamations of liberty, of the rights of Nations to Self-Rule—deepened and strengthened, until it received its sanction in India in 1917, by the declaration of August 20th of that year, which recognised as the aim of British policy the popular ideal. Home Rule, *i.e.*, National Autonomy within the Empire, was the acknowledged object of both, and all seemed fair. But in 1918, at the Special Congress in Bombay, we learned how Sir Michael O'Dwyer's oppressive rule, his persecution of moderate politicians of the educated classes, and his brutal methods of recruitment among the lower, were sowing seeds of hatred which might at any time spring up into action. Then, early in 1919, came the Rowlatt Bills; the withdrawal of one, and the removal of some of the worst features of the other, did little to pacify the exasperated public, who had not imagined that their services in the War and their standing by Britain in the hour of her peril, would be rewarded—after all the show of gratitude—by a new instrument of executive oppression, instead of by the removal of similar measures, which had long placed all lovers of liberty at the mercy of the Executive. At this moment Mr. Gandhi took his first false step, the call for civil disobedience, promising to continue the struggle till the Rowlatt Act was repealed. The Panjab tragedy brought about the breaking of the promise; twice he tried to revive his movement, but gave way at the request of the Government, and he then relinquished it, leaving the Rowlatt Act on the Statute Book.

A new movement began among the Muhammadans in consequence of the tearing away of the European "Turkish Homelands," despite the promise of the British Premier, and "the Ali Brothers" started a semi-religious, semi-political movement against the Indian Government, which had nothing to do with the grievance complained of. Mr. Gandhi joined them, and proposed his new idea of Non-Co-operation. It was to be non-violent, to use only soul-force, violence of language even was forbidden. He had previously surrendered what he said was a principle at the Amritsar Congress, where he was in favour of Co-operation with the Government is consequence of H. M. the King-Emperor's appeal. For the sake of unity he compromised, and acquiesced in a resolution which could be interpreted in opposite senses. Quickly followed the Khilafat agitation, and at the end of May, the All-India Congress Committee decided to call a Special Congress and added the Panjab atrocities to the Khilafat to strengthen the Non-Co-operation movement. It grew and flourished exceedingly, carried all before it at Provincial and District Conferences and at the Special Congress, which expanded the first step of the original fourfold scheme and endorsed the whole of Mr. Gandhi's progressive policy.

Meanwhile Mr. Gandhi had captured the All-India Home Rule League, which had begun to revive its work; he soon changed its name and objects, and now declares that "everything"—Khilafat, Panjab atrocities, all against which Non-Co-operation was originally launched—were "subsidiary to Swarāj". The idea of paralysing the Government has grown into its overthrow; it is to hand over the country to "the people" or vacate it; non-violence has dropped the "non," and we read the most violent epithets, such as Satanic, devilish, applied to it; Mr. Gandhi talks of "when we take up the sword," and he no longer rebukes his followers for using physical violence. He used to fast when they used it; now he condones it. Free Speech has been destroyed, wherever he has a sufficient number of followers to suppress it by violence. The Right of Meeting has gone, where his disciples can break up any in which his methods are exposed. The Right to Vote is taken away by threats of murder, robbery, ruin of business, social boycott, refusal to give food or water to one who claims to use it. The Right to stand for a Legislative Chamber is taken away by similar threats, and the most cowardly of all weapons, the anonymous letter, is used to terrify. The Right to choose one's own diet is denied, and tea-shops are broken into and looted. Non-Co-operation has become a conspiracy against the liberties of the people, in which the most irresponsible elements—children, youths, and ordinary roughs and hooligans—are flung against the citizens. The arch-bureaucrat is now Mr. Gandhi, supported by Messrs. Muhammad and Shaukat Ali. His word is law, and the public is falling back from fear into the state of submission and cowardly obedience from which the Home Rule movement had aroused it. Manliness is disappearing under the new tyranny

The deadliest destruction is that aimed at the education of the young, especially at institutions controlled by Indians, such as the Aligarh and Benares Universities and the Khalsa College; these three, Mr. Gandhi has "no hesitation in saying" must be "destroyed at all costs". In these, so far, the Destroyers have been foiled. Only 30 out of 124 Aligarh Trustees are in favour of spoliation. Mr. Muhammad Ali was to hold the fort in the shape of illegally seized buildings, apparently with the hope of provoking forcible removal, as the youths were told not to leave unless carried away on the shoulders of the evictors; then they would have tried to justify the recourse of violence, not having been the first to use it. But that little plot failed, as the District Magistrate checkmated it. I hope that the Benares authorities will be as firm, despite the strange statement of Pandit Madan Mohan Malaviya on Non-Co-operation; perhaps he was misreported, as I was in Bombay, where I was made to express admiration for Mr. Gandhi!

Having fought for Liberty all my life, I cannot now accept tyranny and a usurped dictatorship. I have not "bowed the knee" in the Temple of Rimmon, and do not propose to do so.

## SUPPRESSION OF FREE SPEECH

THE Suppression of Free Speech is characteristic of all revolutionary movements, as it is of autocracies. The autocrat crushes freedom of speech by coercive legislation, and the revolutionist by terrorism. Lenin and his gang murder men and women who speak or write against the Communist Government. Mr. Gandhi's followers silence them by the brute force of yells and stampings. They easily pass from this to actual physical violence, as was seen outside the theatre at Bombay where they struck the men who accompanied Mrs. Annie Besant to her car. A very little more, and we shall have serious injuries committed by the haters of all liberty, whether of speech, action, or thought. Nor was the mob composed of the rougher classes; the papers naturally call them "hooligans," judging them by their behaviour, but they were well-dressed, many in foreign-cut clothes, and it was only their behaviour that caused them to deserve the epithet. The curious thing is that there is no leaving of Schools and Colleges in Bombay, save by a stray student here and there. They have no reality of conviction, only leathern throats.

It seems, from a summarised article in *The Times of India*, published in our telegraphic columns, that a sapient correspondent blamed Mrs. Besant for inconsistency because she advocated and practised disobedience to the will of the Government in 1917. *The Times* gives an effective reply, pointing out that the circumstances had completely changed. That is true, and as Mr. Lloyd George wittily said, it is foolish "to hammer at an open door". Mrs. Besant hammered at the closed door; now that it is open, she walks through it. But there is another reply. Mrs. Besant did not resist the order of internment, but obeyed it; Mr. Gandhi blamed her at the time for doing so. She claimed Home Rule, but she paid the penalty of her disobedience to Lord Pentland's arbitrary order by submitting to internment. Similarly, she obeyed the orders of externment imposed on her. In order to preserve reverence for Law, while opposing arbitrary commands, it is necessary to suffer the penalty imposed on such opposition, otherwise the ignorant are misled into general disobedience. This is what Mr. Gandhi, in his better days, practised in South Africa. He quietly went to prison and won his cause. So did Mrs. Besant and her colleagues. The proclamation of the decision of the Cabinet of August 20th, 1917, was the result. Had Mrs. Besant refused, to pay the penalty, there would have been rioting, and long delay in the recognition of India's right to Home Rule. It was falsely said the other day, that Mrs. Besant wished the students to strike on her behalf; on the contrary, her representatives, as she was silenced, urged the students to take no action, maintaining the policy she had always taught.

We deeply regret that Mr. Eardley Norton, whose services to India are so well known, was very rudely treated during his lecture on Monday at Gokhale Hall. Students, encouraged by Mr. Gandhi in disobedience, are naturally tyrants, and want to rule their elders. It is he, not they, who are to blame. India is likely to be a very miserable country when these young men become mature and rule the land, for they are sure to continue the intolerance they now show.

Mr. Gandhi who, according to the report of his speech at Poona, said that he was in favour of the caste-system and only objected to "untouchability," is also said to have attacked an (imaginary) conspiracy of Brahmanas to outcaste Panchamas, and dubbed Brahmanas "satanic". He apparently forgets that it is Brahmanas who have long striven to uplift the outcastes, and non-Brahmanas, especially on the West Coast, who have concerted action to oppress them. It will be seen from the note below that having thus set the example of abuse, and done his best to embitter still further non-Brahmana feeling, he asked them not to abuse Brahmanas! Example would be better than precept.

One good note has been struck, the first result of the new movement in Bombay. A large meeting has been held in Surat, where Sir Chimanlal Setalwad, M.L.A., the Hon. Mr. Purshottamdas Thakurdas (Sheriff of Bombay) and Mr. Jamnadas Dwarkadas, M.L.A., delivered addresses against Non-Co-operation to a deeply interested audience. We understand they propose to visit other towns, and cordially wish them success.

---

## NON-CO-OPERATION AND LABOUR

THE policy of this paper in reference to Labour disputes is well-known. We do not favour strikes or lock-outs. We stand for arbitration, and arrangements mutually arrived at by opposing parties. Our views on Non-Co-operation are also familiar to the public. We see in Mr. Gandhi's movement a grave danger to peace and order in the country. There is one point to which we wish to draw the special attention of the authorities and all concerned, as a result of our recent experience in Bombay and elsewhere.

There are a great number of strikes and lock-outs going on, at the present time, all over India, thus throwing thouands upon thousands of labourers out in the streets, workless and restless. We have reasons to believe that a nefarious propaganda is being carried on in their midst by interested people. Election time, in any country, produces restlessness; in India, at present, more than election restlessness prevails. To add to this undesirable situation a further and more turbulent kind of restlessness of unemployed labour, skilled or unskilled, is rank folly. And yet, in Calcutta, Jhansi, Bombay, Madras, and elsewhere, thousands of work-people are driven out to roam free, to be made a catspaw of, by the ever-watchful Non-Co-operator.

We are not here concerned with the rights or wrongs of any strike or lock-out; all that we want to point out to the Government is the seriousness of the situation, for we think that sharp political propaganda is being carried on among the labourers. Apart from the fact that among the labour leaders there are staunch Non-Co-operators, we must not overlook the fact that Mr. Gandhi is well-nigh worshipped by the labourers in all big cities, for they do not quite understand the inwardness of the movement which he is leading. Under the circumstances, it seems to us to be a bad blunder for employers to allow their men to be out in the streets. During the recent strikes in Bombay, for instance, we were given to understand a very good propaganda was carried on by the Non-Co-operators, and, what is worse, by friends of violence in the name of Non-Co-operation.

A particular strike or lock-out may be right or wrong; we are not concerned with that. What we want to point out is that the Government ought not to permit strikes and lock-outs to continue for any length of time. For example, who can tell us what the postmen on strike in Bombay have been listening to and thinking about, and what they are after, outside their own strike work? There are troubles in Malabar, and constant labour rows in Madras. It is a well-known fact that the Government has influence with employers of labour, and we are of opinion that they ought to interfere at a very early stage, and, even at the risk of being dubbed partial to a contending party, bring about an amicable settlement. Their business at present, at any rate till the elections are over, is to see that labourers are not out of employment. As we feel that the situation all over India in regard to labour is very critical, we hope the Government will attend to this matter with the least possible delay.

## THE HINDU UNIVERSITY ATTACKED

It is a pity that Non-Co-operators are so indifferent to truth, where their remarkable form of "soul-force" is appealed to. It seems that, according to the account in the *Hindu*, the Secretary of the "Benares Hindu University Non-Co-operation Committee" informs the credulous public that:

> On the pressing invitation of the Benares Hindu University, who had sent their representatives to Ghazipur, Doctor Ansari and Pandit Jawahirlal Nehru came to Benares on the 17th November.

This is a glaring falsehood. The Hindu University, it is needless to say, sent no invitation to the Destroyers. Presumably, the invitation was sent by the abovenamed Committee, and it is clearly the duty of the Principal of the College to put an end to this shameful abuse of the name of the Hindu University. Mr. Bhagwati Pershad Mitra, presumably a College student, should be informed that a stray student cannot use the name of the University to cover his foolish actions. It is part of the bluff by which the Gandhians try to deceive the country. We are told that, according to the *Aj*, of which Mr. Shri Prakasha is Editor, some students applied to the Principal for permission to hold a meeting for Non-Co-operation within the College precincts, to listen to the enemies of education, and it was very properly refused. Enemies besieging a fortress can only be admitted by traitors.

Dr. Ansari said that the University was in no sense National, and that it could not move a finger without the sanction of the Head of the Local Government. That is absolutely false. The control is in the hands of the University Court, all the members of which are Hindus, except Mrs. Annie Besant. The Government subscribes a lakh annually out of money raised from the people, and no conditions are attached to the grant. The Central Hindu College, the nucleus of the University, never received a pie from Government. Dr. Ansari was equally far from the truth when he said that it was through institutions like the Hindu University that the Government exercised control over the people, for the Hindu University was unique until a short time ago, when the Muslim University was chartered.

Babu Shiva Prasad Gupta said that the students should either nationalise the University or leave it. May one be permitted to ask what "nationalise" in this connection means? Only a law, and a Government carrying it out, can nationalise anything. Certainly the buildings cannot be appropriated by the students, since the law protects them, and the students, if ordered by the University authorities to leave, would, if they remained, become guilty of criminal trespass, as Mr. Muhammad Ali found out the other day, when the District Magistrate explained the position to him. Happily, the wished for state of anarchy does not yet exist; only when the Non-Co-operators have produced anarchy, will people be able to take possession of other people's goods. Then the approbation of the Non-Co-operator will probably depend on whether he is the seizer of other people's goods, or a more muscular Non-Co-operator is the seizer of his. Mr. Gandhi should disorganise the police, before his followers begin rioting and robbery. Until then, they must follow Mr. Muhammad Ali's example and leave the premises.

Pandit Motilal Nehru added to the honours so freely showered on the Government by calling it "damnable".

Pandit Madan Mohan Malaviya was lying ill and forbidden to see anyone, while the institution for which he has worked so well was being attacked. But the failure in Benares will be even worse than at Aligarh.

Even in Ahmedabad the Gandhian movement meets with little success, and the Government has been obliged to relax its rule against overcrowding, in order to accommodate the students who are leaving the institutions which have abandoned Government grants and affiliation to the Government University. So he has only succeeded in driving some boys out of "national" into Government institutions.

It is clear that the reports sent to the papers by Non-Co-operators are not reliable. We had from a private source an account of the visit to Satara very different from that which appeared in the papers, and the disappointments of the tour may be the reason for the increased violence of Mr. Gandhi's language.

---

## NOTES

### PLEDGES

Much obloquy is poured upon the British Prime Minister for the breaking of his promise about Thrace remaining a part of the Turkish Empire. The leading trio, Mr. Gandhi and Messrs. Muhammad and Shaukat Ali, are never tired of reiterating that Mr. Lloyd George is "perjured". But when the Principal of the Aligarh College reminded Mr. Gandhi of *his* promise that he would not seek to interfere with the College students at Aligarh, he airily stated that he had changed his view and that the students must be sacrificed. A promise, then, is binding on Mr. Lloyd George but not on Mr. Gandhi; Mr. Lloyd George is a "perjurer," while Mr. Gandhi is a "saint". It may well be said that love is blind, but we do not think that a man who breaks a promise has any right to reproach another promise-breaker. Does Mr. Gandhi think that truth, like the students, must be sacrificed to the "higher politics"?

### MR. GANDHI'S PROPAGANDA AMONG STUDENTS

Mr. Gandhi's brief letter to the students of Wilson College, Bombay, with no other object than to "be of some help in enabling them to solve the question" of the boycott, should finally dispose of the possibility of misinterpreting his intentions, wilful or otherwise. It has been suggested by responsible Non-Co-operators, if such a contradiction in terms be permitted for the occasion, that Mr. Gandhi hopes to reform the educational system in the country through his National institutions, and that the boycott is only to be gradual. After referring to the various sins of the Government in the letter above alluded to, Mr. Gandhi proceeds: "I have, therefore, no hesitation in saying that it is sinful for us to receive education in schools and colleges conducted by or through it" (the Government). And, says he finally, which is the real point of our contention, "it is better to be without such education or even to suspend it till we have received redress".

## Mr. Gandhi's Panjab Tour

Interesting sidelight is thrown by the Lahore correspondent of *The Bombay Chronicle*, on the lukewarm enthusiasm Mr. Gandhi's last Panjab tour evoked even amongst those who have, according to him, handed over the honour of their faith into his custody. He was expected to be in Lahore on Dusserah day. But Muslim institutions, wiser after the Aligarh event, preferred to give their students a holiday, apparently contrary to their usual custom. Whether this was in order to prevent Mr. Gandhi from having an opportunity of inculcating "higher politics" into impulsive youths, or due to a growing friendly spirit between Hindus and Muslims, the correspondent is unable to say. But the result of the step undoubtedly was that large numbers of the students of the Islamia College were not in Lahore during the period of Mr. Gandhi's stay. His discourse on "higher politics" to the privileged few who remained does not seem to have convinced even this correspondent, whose belief in the movement is, nevertheless, deep and unshaken. Mr. Gandhi trotted out his phrases about the vicious system of education, Swarāj being a path of sacrifice and renunciation, matters of conscience, etc. It was their duty, he told them, to disobey their parents. The correspondent's comments on the speech are instructive:

Whatever the logical merits of Mr. Gandhi's argument to the students may be, it is not apparent that he took pains to make the students realise the meaning and the import of the words "higher politics," and one very much suspects that it was only another instance of an old idea appearing in the garb of a new phrase, and the subtle meaning of the Satyāgraha doctrine does not become more obvious to the crowd by its new terminology. One is not convinced that Mr. Gandhi has captured the students by any process of intellectual reasoning. What he undoubtedly has done is to capture the imaginations of the student community.

This does not sound like appreciation, and coming from one of his own followers is significant.

### "Crores of Lives"

Mr. Gandhi is now proclaiming, not only that the Government is a Satanic Government, which must apologise for the Panjab atrocities, and redress the Khilafat injustices—which it has no power to do—or else it was the people's foremost duty to destroy them; he also says that to gain Swarāj "he was prepared to sacrifice crores of lives, if he could be assured of success". "Crores" must be at least two, so twenty million lives, at least, Mr. Gandhi is prepared to sacrifice. And a little time ago he would go to the Himālayas if Moulana Shaukat Ali took up the sword! No wonder young men are stirred to madness when a senior talks in this mad and wicked way. The disciple of Ahimsa has, indeed, changed. We had heard that he had been speaking on this line to his friends, but had not expected to see it in print.

# APPENDIX

[These articles appeared in *New India*, written by Mrs. Annie Besant on April 15, 16, 20 and 21, 1920.]

## CO-OPERATION OR NON-CO-OPERATION

I AM deeply grieved to see that, at the second sitting of the All-India Khilafat Committee, it was decided not only that Non-Co-operation with the Government should be adopted, but that a time was fixed for the beginning of this method—the official declaration of the Treaty with Turkey. The Sub-Committee which presented the report containing this unfortunate recommendation consisted of Mr. Gandhi, Moulana Shaukat Ali, and Moulana Abdul Kalam Azad. A rule passed later laid down:

> That all Provincial and other Khilafat Committees should not pass any resolution against the principles laid down by the All-India Khilafat Committee, as their existence is for the purpose of promulgating the objects laid down by the Central Khilafat Committee.

This being so, we must presume that the Madras meeting, like the meeting lately held at Bombay, will call on all Indians to refuse Co-operation with the Government. This means in plain language, though the Committee may not have meant it, to call on all Indians to abandon all work under the Reform Act, except for candidates who will refuse to co-operate with the Government, and will thus ensure the wrecking of the Act. Under these circumstances, no one who loves India better than he loves the Turkish Empire can work with the All-India Khilafat Committee. Their Deputation in London has demanded the restoration of Turkey to her status before the War. Britain has no power to do this, being but one of the Allies and with America, France and Italy against her. Mr. Montagu has done his utmost and the Premier has his Cabinet practically cloven in twain. Is it just, is it fair, to ask all Indians to withdraw from all Co-operation with a Government which has tried to gain for the Musalmans the utmost that can be obtained for them?

We know that Mr. Gandhi does not care much about political reforms in general and the Reform Act in particular. He gave the weight of his name to the Amritsar declaration that it was inadequate, unsatisfactory and disappointing, and he withdrew his amendment promising Co-operation with the officials in its working. He therefore cannot be blamed for sacrificing the Reforms out of his love for his Musalman brethren, and his eagerness to preserve the Entente between them and the Hindus. The probable result will be to divide the ranks once more, into Co-operating Hindus-Musalmans, and Non-Co-operating Hindus-Musalmans. A cleavage which paralysed political life in Bombay for a year and sadly crippled the reform deputations in England was caused by the Satyāgraha movement last year; apparently a similar course will again paralyse it this year, just as it is reviving and taking up active work.

Apart from this stimulus to new cleavages and consequent paralysis, what does Non-Co-operation mean, if it is real? Real it will *not* be, but only a matter of passing empty resolutions for the many and the plunging into misery and want of a few brave men and their families.

If it were real, all Government servants would resign their situations, and the Government would be paralysed. All Indian soldiers and police would abandon their duties, and the predatory classes would enjoy an orgy of looting. All Municipal and Local Boards of every sort would dissolve, their officers and staffs would cease to function, and chaos would ensue, followed by pestilence. All State railways would be without servants, transport would cease, food supplies would be stopped. The Indian staffs of schools, colleges and universities would leave their duties. And all this without any preparation to supply the immense void thus created. Sir Edward Carson, when he contemplated such a paralysis of the King's Government over a small portion of Ireland, had at least the foresight to provide a Provincial Government beforehand, ready to step into the place of the paralysed authorities, to drill an army to keep order, and generally to prepare for the change aimed at with the least cost to the population concerned. But here no preparations have been made to safeguard a population of 315,000,000 of people over the vast area from the Himālayas to Cape Comorin. Naturally, the answer will be: "All these things will not happen." Quite so. But that means that the resolutions are empty bluff, and that those who pass them do not mean to carry them out. A few will cease to co-operate; there may be a few riots as there were last year, some families bereft of their dear ones, some persons imprisoned, race-hatred indefinitely increased. The utter failure of 1919 to do anything effective might have taught a lesson to 1920. Let us hope that the failure will be even more complete, that not one man will lose his life, be wounded, or sent to gaol. That is the best that can happen.

It is quite possible that the All-India Khilafat Committee has never thought of studying "Non-Co-operation" from this standpoint. But they must mean *something*. Is it not their duty to say publicly what they do mean? Do they trust to the general indifference to prevent any effect being given to the resolutions which are to be passed? There seems little understanding here of what can be done and what cannot be done by agitation through public meetings. Meetings may appeal to a Government to do or not to do a particular thing, and these will be effective or ineffective according as the Government judges that they do, or do not, represent a large measure of public opinion. But meetings appealing to the people to do some definite thing can only be effective if a large number of the people do the thing. In this case, if they do what they are asked to do, the above results would follow. If they do not, the resolutions are ridiculed, and the Government goes on its way unheeding. A man needs to be very sure of his followers before he asks them to *act*.

Under present circumstances many of us are placed in a very painful position. We will no more follow Mr. Gandhi in his present course than we would follow him last year, for his present policy is even more dangerous than that of 1919, which ended so disastrously. Many of us who honour Messrs. Shaukat Ali and Muhammad Ali—and who worked for them during their long years of suffering a good deal harder than most of those who will meet and cheer them to-morrow—are shut out from the welcome to them because we believe that their present policy, if successful, will be fatal to the Commonwealth, if unsuccessful, as it will be, will be harmful to Islam, to the Khilafat and to themselves. It will also injure the neo-Nationalists, either by creating a cleavage among them or by hopelessly discrediting them, and while I hope to see them in a minority in the coming elections, I do not want to see them thoroughly discredited, for in a Nation's progress to Liberty those who cry out for the impossible render the attainment of the possible nearer than it would otherwise be.

---

## CONSCIENCE

In the present condition of the Khilafat Question, a difference of opinion has arisen as to the adoption of Non-Co-operation as a means of pressure on the Government. On this, opinion is divided even among Musalmans, some of whom hold, while others do not, that it is incumbent on all who hold the Faith of Islam to refuse to recognise and help a Government which does not insist on the Musalman demand being conceded by the Allies. In order to increase this pressure, Mr. Gandhi has asked all non-Muslim Indians to join their Muslim brethren in their renouncal of Co-operation. On this, I wrote yesterday, and there is no need to repeat the arguments used. I regard the resolution as impracticable, as dangerous if local attempts are made to carry it out, and as one to which no non-Musalman citizen should adhere.

For the Musalman, everything turns on the mandate of his own conscience, when he has decided that his Faith commands him, or does not command him, to choose between his allegiance to the Khalifa and his allegiance to the Crown. In the latter case, he is evidently free to support the Khalifa by every means in his power short of breaking his allegiance to the Crown. It may be remembered that Mr. Muhammad Ali once said that if the Turks invaded India, he would fight against them, though they were under the command of the Khalifa, in defence of his native land. It would therefore seem that a good Musalman may actively resist the Khalifa in obedience to the higher call of Patriotism, although in such case he would support the Crown and defy the Khalifa. It is clear that the question of which of the two allegiances is supreme, is a question for the Musalman only, not for the non-Musalman, to decide.

But suppose that this is a question not of allegiance to the Khalifa, but of obedience to the command of the Prophet Muhammad—on whom be blessing—himself? If the question takes that form, then I can only say that a man's own conscience is the supreme judge of the man's actions, and that, however much one may dissent from his conclusion, one must respect his conscientious decision, and honour him for his courage in asserting and carrying it out. The early Christians were in just that position. A pinch of incense, burnt before the statue of Cæsar, was accepted as the proof that they acknowledged him as Divine. They died rather than burn it, were executed for treason to the State. To my mind, they deserve honour as martyrs, quite apart from the rightness or wrongness of their faith. Men and women who are ready to renounce all, life, liberty, property, rather than deny their conscience, lift and purify society, and are worthy of all honour. Hence, while refusing to accept Non-Co-operation, while earnestly dissuading all non-Musalmans whom I can influence from accepting it, while seeking to persuade Musalmans who do not hold it as "of faith" to stand apart from it, I can say no word of persuasion to those who hold that their Islamic faith commands them to offer this form of "passive resistance". They "can no other".

The Khilafat Committee have very kindly invited me to their Conference, and I intend to go: first, because I want to hear the strongest arguments that can be advanced in favour of what I believe to be wrong; secondly, because I want to show sympathy with the Musalmans, suffering so sorely and so long under the lessening power of their Sovereign States; thirdly, because Britain is unable to perform the pledge given by her Premier, and thus inflicts, however involuntarily, a wrong on her Musalman citizens; and lastly, because I honour a man who has suffered confinement unjustly for five long years, and would show him honour in the hour of his peril as a Confessor of his Faith, when that Faith is out of the sunshine. When a man says with full conviction: "I must obey God rather than man," all who believe in God should say "Amen".

# THE PRESENT CRISIS

We have now arrived at a stage in the question of the Khilafat the gravity of which cannot be overestimated. It is stated that the Peace Conference has refused to receive the Muslim Deputation, and that Mr. Gandhi is therefore leaving at once to represent Hindu views in Europe. Hindu views are exceedingly divided on the Non-Co-operation resolution of Mr. Gandhi, and it would not be justifiable to represent that resolution as embodying the general Hindu view. Large numbers doubtless will follow Mr. Gandhi's lead, but larger numbers will probably dissent from it, as even the Musalmans themselves are by no means agreed on the forms of Non-Co-operation laid down. Despite the inspiring presence of Moulana Shaukat Ali in Madras, the Conference here only accepted four stages, and dropped the final step, stopping short of his final logical conclusion of the independence of India.

The resolution embodying the four stages, as passed by the Conference, ran:

> In consonance with the spirit of the resolution adopted by the All-India Committee, this Conference, in the event of the present agitation proving futile and ineffective, calls upon all Indians to resort to progressive abstention from Co-operation with Government in the following manner:
>
> Firstly, to renounce all honorary posts, titles and membership of Legislative Councils;
>
> Secondly, to give up all remunerative posts under Government service;
>
> Thirdly, to give up all appointments in the Police and Military forces; and
>
> Fourthly, to refuse to pay taxes to Government.

Five Hindu leaders of the neo-Nationalists pledged themselves to this resolution: Mr. Kasturiranga Iyengar who seconded it, Messrs. Satyamurti, A. Rangaswami Iyengar, M. K. Acharya and C. Rajagopalachari, who supported it. The latter added that "if there were any Hindus or Musalmans who for want of courage lagged behind, they would be the cause of the misery of future generations". Hindus and Musalmans who object to these resolutions are not necessarily motived by want of courage. The majority of Hindus and Musalmans have none of the things which the first, second, and third clauses call on them to renounce, so they can take the pledge with a light heart, if they are blind to consequences. The fourth will test their courage. So far as No. 1 is concerned, the Government will be in no way troubled if it is carried out. There will be plenty of people to fill the vacated seats, and plenty of candidates for the rejected honours. No. 2, if carried out, would paralyse the administration, while No. 3 would give a good time to the criminal classes. The danger does not lie in these clauses, but in the spirit behind them—the almost certainty of riots, of murderous attacks on those who disagree with, and decline to take part in, or oppose, the propaganda for reducing society into its component parts. Musalmans who feel these things to be their religious duty are bound to do them, but they have no right to call on those who have no such religious duty, or who dissent from this view of their duty if they are Muslims, to run amok at society, and reduce it to anarchy. If they should succeed in paralysing the police and the army, are they ready to preserve our towns from pillage, our women from rape, our men from murder by the ruffians found in every land? Are they ready to guard our frontiers from the wild hill tribes, the tribes of Central Asia, and the Pathans of Afghanistan? Are Messrs. Kasturiranga Iyengar and the other four gentlemen prepared to drill police and soldiers to guard even Madras from riot and disorder?

They may say that there is no danger, because the Government will give way before their menace. We doubt it. These proposed stages lead directly to the establishment of Indian independence by revolution, and it is idle to blink the fact. They mean the reduction of India to the state of Russia.

And this is done at a moment when every energy should be bent to the gaining of power by the means placed in our hands, to the uplift of India by education, by industrial and agricultural improvement, by wise use of National resources, by putting an end to the conditions that reduce the average age of our people to 23·5 years. Everything that has been gained by thirty-five years of work and sacrifice is to be thrown into the melting pot, in order to plunge into a whirlpool of struggle and inevitable ruin to India, be the victory on which side it may. Asia, not India only, is endangered by the invasion of

European Powers, with their annexations, their mandates, their unjust and arrogant claims. Eastern civilisation and culture are imperilled, and with them, the future of humanity. All the resources of science are in the hands of the West. What has the East to oppose to them? Can they create arms, aeroplanes, guns with a range of 150 miles, in a few weeks? To face the danger of the submergence of Asian culture we need careful preparation, full consultation, the help of our wisest and best, the uniting of all Asian Nations in a defensive League against western exploitation and annexation.

The touch of comedy in this menace of tragedy, tragedy invited by hasty and dangerous methods devised by a few and thoughtlessly accepted by many, is the fact that the neo-Nationalists who join the movement are by their own pledge shut out from the Councils!

---

## A TRUE SATYĀGRAHI

By Annie Besant

Mr. C. Rajagopalachariar's speech at the Khilafat meeting yesterday was profoundly interesting, partly because it was a self-revelation, and partly because it evoked a self-revelation by the audience. It is therefore worthy of respectful consideration, for controversy carried on in the spirit shown by him must be instructive to the readers, if not to the combatants themselves.

I do not think that I fail to understand either the justice of the Khilafat cause or the depth of the Musalman feeling theranent. I think that the non-carrying out of the Premier's pledge is unjust and inflicts a real wrong on the Musalmans of India, who, as Mr. Lloyd George admitted, were led by it to go in large numbers into the army which fought against the Sultan, their Khalifa. Such a pledge was a pledge of honour, and is not redeemed by leaving the Sultan in Constantinople under the Allied guns, nor by tearing away from him Thrace and the Turkish Homelands. If I did not, at least to some extent, realise the depth of Musalman feeling, I should be indifferent to the four steps, steps which inevitably lead to the breaking of the connection between India and Britain. It is because I feel its depth and reality, that I fear that ruin to India will result from these steps.

I said that "Hindu views are exceedingly divided on the Non-Co-operation resolution of Mr. Gandhi, and it would not be justifiable to represent that resolution as embodying the general Hindu view". Mr. Rajagopalachari says that is not Mr. Gandhi's programme; he is only going to say they are "not divided on the Khilafat question". But surely the Non-Co-operation declared by the All-India Khilafat Conference and endorsed by Bombay and Madras is a vital and integral part of the Khilafat question. If it is not, I am thankful, for my objections are levelled against that, and not generally against the "question," on which I have shown sympathy and tried to help. I trust Mr. Gandhi will make it plain that he is not going to lecture on that, nor advocate it. I thought he was pressing Hindus to adopt Non-Co-operation, and I was writing on that, and not on the general question, as my words show. I grant also that if anyone agrees with the resolution, it would be want of courage not to act on it. I utterly disagree with it, and dread the riot and bloodshed that will follow, if it is acted on widely. If No. 1 is innocuous and does not "trouble Government," it is merely futile, since the declared object is to put pressure on Government.

Mr. Rajagopalachari then urges that the withdrawal from police will not lead to pillage and the rest. Does he really think that people who, on a question of vital interest deserving of deep thought, utter the cries which he rebuked are capable of sublime self-control? They cannot even control their tongues and their tempers, nor endure a grave difference of opinion without flinging insults at anyone with whom they disagree. And below them is the criminal population found in every large city. That will yield the murderers, the looters, the firers of buildings, who will be loosed on our defenceless cities. The "police force would not be necessary". If it were necessary it "would be there". How? by the untrained young men? They "would drill themselves to maintain order"; and by the time they were drilled, the cities would be destroyed and the citizens murdered.

As to foreign invasion, the British Government should defend the country. But how and with what? The Hindus and Musalmans will have deserted. Only the English officers and soldiers will be left—a mere handful. The crowd laughed at the idea of invasion. They may think differently when they have paralysed the army, and Pathans and Afghans are murdering and looting in their streets.

I would rather not comment on the concluding sentences. They hint at a catastrophe better undiscussed.

I thank Mr. Rajagopalachari for his speech. As to the shouters, I am used to them, and he said nothing to incite, but met them with rebuke. Would that all professed Satyāgrahis were like him.

---

### Sir C. Setalvad Interviewed

Bombay, November 6.—Interviewed by a representative of the Associated Press regarding the present political situation in India, Sir Chimanlal Setalvad, at the outset, referred to the breaking up of Mrs. Besant's lecture on Thursday, and said it was fully expected, as threats had been openly given on the previous day, that Thursday's meeting would be made impossible. There was a large number of people who resented such tactics and wanted to hear Mrs. Besant, but they rightly refused to follow the example of the rowdy element and bring about a conflict. Sir Chimanlal, continuing, said that he was very glad the exhibition which the Non-Co-operators made of themselves; for it conclusively demonstrated certain dangers and the disastrous consequences of the Non-Co-operation propaganda. We have been crying out, he said, against the suppression of the liberty of speech and freedom of the Press by Government through the Press Act, Seditious Meetings Act and similar legislation; but if what happened on Thursday is an indication, there would be complete suppression of liberty of speech under the Swarāj which Mr. Gandhi is going to achieve in a few months. I wonder if Mr. Gandhi feels proud of those who shouted his "Jai," although there is nothing surprising in it, as those who committed arson and murdered innocent men during the 1919 disturbances did so shouting, "Gandhi-ki-Jai". I have no doubt the Non-Co-operation programme will lead the country into disaster, but I am sure the common sense of the public will, in the end, prevail.

After referring to the danger existing, owing to hatred being created between Europeans and Indians and among Indians themselves, and to the folly of neglecting the great opportunities for administration and directing the policy placed in the hands of the people under the Reform Scheme, Sir Chimanlal dealt with Mr. Gandhi's policy, and said that the only item adopted, in a measure, in certain parts of the country, is the boycott of Councils, which really requires no sacrifice, as it saves Non-Co-operators the time and trouble they would otherwise be obliged to devote to the Councils. It was noteworthy in this connection that, at the All-India Trade Union Congress, Lala Lajput Rai and others, who favoured the boycott, joined in the resolutions demanding Council representation for Labour and sending a deputation to the Governor. The movement for lawyers to give up practice had failed miserably. The boycott of schools was the most dangerous and mischievous item of the programme. Under the Reform Scheme there may be ample opportunity and scope for an Indian Minister to remedy the defects of the present system of Education, but Mr. Gandhi wanted to scrap all the existing educational institutions with their many crores spent on capital expenditure, and turn all students adrift. He is going to provide National Schools, Colleges and Universities, but one does not know how he is going to get the necessary crores for initial expenditure and crores to carry on the work every year. What distresses one most is the way the Muhammadans are going to suffer. They only recently realised the importance of education, and had been making earnest efforts to pick up; but if Mr. Gandhi prevails, the clock of Muhammadan educational progress would be set back by fifty years. Mr. Gandhi is prepared to teach the youth of the country to despise and disobey parents and teachers, however much such a course may be contrary to Indian traditions and subversive of the foundations of society. I am convinced that the Non-Co-operation propaganda must lead to violence and anarchy, and will put back, for many years, the attainment of Self-Government, which can only be achieved by self-restraint, self-discipline and hard work.

Sir Chimanlal then observed that it was necessary to enquire why Mr. Gandhi secured whatever success he had achieved, why had India, which stood like one man by the British Empire during the war, so changed that Mr. Gandhi's doctrine of hate fell on receptive ears. The Government must face this question squarely, and a solution must be found. It is obvious, he said, India's self-respect has been wounded by the doings in the Panjab, the mishandling of the Khilafat question and the treatment of Indians in the British Dominions, and a feeling of despair has come over the people. Until the root causes are removed, it is extremely difficult, if not impossible, to make the people realise the dangers of Mr. Gandhi's campaign. It is in the interests of Britain and India that the wounds, from which India is suffering, should be healed, and the feeling of mutual confidence and trust be restored, by which alone Britain and India, marching together in equal comradeship, can work out their great destiny. I do hope and trust that British statesmanship will grasp the situation, and set to work to effect the desired results without delay.

---

## GOVERNMENT OF INDIA'S RESOLUTION

SIMLA, November 6.—A *Gazette of India Extraordinary* issued to-day publishes the following Resolution by the Government of India in the Home Department:

In view of the recent events, the Governor-General-in-Council considers that it is necessary to make a further declaration of the attitude and policy of the Government of India towards the Non-Co-operation movement not only for the guidance of Local Governments and Administrations, but also for the information of the people of India. At the opening of the autumn session of the Imperial Legislative Council, H. E. the Viceroy explained the policy which the Government of India have up to date followed in this matter. Although, in their opinion, the movement is unconstitutional, in that it has, as its object, the paralysis and subversion of the existing administration of the country, the Government have hitherto refrained from instituting criminal proceedings or taking any other action against those of its promoters who have advocated, simultaneously with Non-Co-operation, abstention from violence, and they have instructed Local Governments to take action against those persons only who, in furtherance of the movement, have gone beyond the limits originally set by its organisers, and have, by speech or writing, openly incited the public to violence, or have attempted to tamper with the loyalty of the Army or of the Police. In adopting this policy, the Government have been influenced by several consideration. In the first place, they have been reluctant to interfere with the liberty of speech and the freedom of the press at a time when India is on the threshold of a great advance towards the realisation of the principle of Self-Government within the Empire, when, indeed, the first elections are already in sight in recognition of that advance; and in pursuance of the spirit of the King-Emperor's Proclamation of December last, they extended His Majesty's clemency to many hundreds of political offenders who were then in custody, and they have since released from the restrictions of the Press Act numerous papers which were formerly held to security. Although these concessions have in many cases failed to evoke any response or recognition, Government are loth to reimpose the restrictions which have so lately been relaxed. In the second place, the Government are at all times reluctant to embark on a campaign against individuals, some of whom may be actuated by honest, if misguided, motives. This consideration is reinforced by the knowledge that such action, even if it took the form of prosecution under the ordinary criminal law, would be likely to give those against whom it might be directed the opportunity of posing as martyrs and might also, by evoking false sympathy, swell the number of adherents to a cause which has in itself no intrinsic merit to commend it to public acceptance. The third and chief consideration, however, which has influenced the Government of India is their trust in the commonsense of India, their belief that the sanity of the classes and the masses alike would reject Non-Co-operation as a visionary and chimerical scheme which, if successful, could only result in widespread disorder, political chaos and the ruin of all those who have any real stake in the country. The appeal of Non-Co-operation is to prejudice and ignorance, and its creed is devoid of any constructive genius. India has had bitter experience of the fruits of its forerunner, the Satyāgraha cult, and the Governor-General in Council still hopes that, with that lamentable warning before her eyes, India will reject the much greater peril of Non-Co-operation. Its principal exponents have firmly avowed that their object is to destroy the present Government, to dig up the foundations of the British Government in India, and they have promised their followers that if only their gospel be generally accepted, India shall be self-governing and independent within one year. The full consummation of their hopes would leave India defenceless alike against foreign aggression and internal chaos. The benefits of stable Government and undisturbed peace, the results that have been attained by the orderly progress of India for more than a century, the still greater results which, it is hoped, will attend her advance under the Reform Scheme, her material prosperity and her political progress, are all to be sacrificed to the irresponsible caprice of a few misguided men. The confidence of Government in the good sense of India has already been in a great measure justified by the unanimity of her best minds in their condemnation of the folly of Non-Co-operation. For a most weighty body of educated opinion has rejected this new doctrine as one that is fraught with most mischievous potentialities for India. But having failed to secure a favourable verdict from Educated India, the leaders of the movement have now been driven to increase the violence of their appeal to the masses, and to endeavour to enlist, under the banner of Non-Co-operation, the sympathy and assistance of immature schoolboys and College students. Herein lie two great dangers for India which have compelled the Government to place the issues plainly before the country in the hope that its most enlightened and stable elements may clearly recognise the necessity of vigorous and united action to prevent further extention of the mischief. Of these two latest developments, the most immoral is undoubtedly the mischievous attack which has been made on the youth of the country, who are to be sacrificed to the exigencies of a political campaign. It matters not to the leaders of the movement if the foundations of home life are sapped and children set against their parents and teachers, provided their own ends are attained and the success of their campaign assured. The appeal to the illiterate and the ignorant is also fraught with very grave danger. It has already resulted in at least one deplorable crime, and it is certain that the restless activity of the leaders, who wander from one city to another stirring up excitement amongst the masses by inflammatory speeches, and by the reiteration of false statements despite constant contradiction, may at any moment result in serious outbreaks of disorder. The best weapon to combat both dangers lies in the practical help and sympathy of sober-minded and moderate men, and the Government therefore call on all who have the good of India at heart to organise themselves and take concerted measures to assist the cause of law and order by active opposition to the movement, by the exercise of their influence over the minds of the ignorant and the immature, and by public exposure and denunciation of the evils of Non-Co-operation and of the anarchy to which it must inevitably lead. The Government appreciate the action which has already been taken in this direction by men of liberal opinion and moderate mind throughout India, and they congratulate the country more particularly on the manifestations of public displeasure which have occurred in regard to the mischievous attack on Education. The opposition which has been offered to this phase of the movement by the Trustees of the M.A.O. College at Aligarh, by the authorities of the Khalsa College at Amritsar, by many other school authorities, by the great majority of teachers and parents, and also by large sections of the student community itself is, indeed, a most hopeful feature in the situation. The Government realise that it is to enlightened public opinion they must chiefly trust for the dissipation of the danger that now envelops India, as it is on that same public opinion that India's political future must depend. It is in this trust that they have refrained in the past, so far as is consistent with public safety, from repressive action, for they consider that such action should only be employed in the last resort when, indeed, failure to adopt it would be a criminal betrayal of the people. How long with due regard to their ultimate responsibility for the public safety the Government will be able to maintain that policy, will depend largely on the success which attends the efforts of the moderate citizens to check the extension of the movement and keep its dangers within bounds.

# CONCLUSION

## By Their Fruits Ye shall Know Them

The bitter fruits of the Tree of Hate planted by Mr. Gandhi and his two Muhammadan friends are setting on edge the teeth of the people. Rights of Free Speech, of Free Meeting, of Free Vote, of Free Election are assailed; Education is interfered with; disobedience to parents and teachers is openly preached; trade is interfered with; even tea-shops are looted; the Government is assailed as Satanic, devilish, inhuman, cruel, damnable; it is to be destroyed; crores of lives may be sacrificed. Such are the present teachings of the apostle of non-violence. He began as a dove of peace, but has become a destroyer.

All lovers of peace and order, of liberty and progress, should unite to oppose this fatal propaganda, which began with professions of peace and is now naked violence. It is up to good citizens of every rank, caste and creed to join hands against a movement which has so rapidly changed its character from peace to a declaration of war. This is not the business of the Government, but the business of the Nation, obstructed on every hand by those who are paralysing its activities.

Printed by J. R. Aria at the Vasanta Press, Adyar, Madras.